Also by Elizabeth N. Doyd

Write Him Off: Heal Your Broken Heart in 30 Days

The Love Book: Writing Your Way to Your Soul Mate

Gratitude Journal: 52 Writing Prompts to Celebrate Your Wonderful Life

7 Days to Minimalistic Living: A Stress-Free Guide to Declutter, Clean and Organize Your Home and Your Life

The Science of Getting Rich

Action Plan

Wallace D. Wattles
Elizabeth N. Doyd

Copyright © 2014 by Elizabeth N. Doyd

All rights reserved.

No part of this publication may be reproduced, distributed or transmitted in any form or by any means, including photocopying, recording, or any other electronic or mechanical methods, without the prior written permission of the publisher, except in the case of brief quotations embodied in critical reviews and certain other noncommercial uses permitted by copyright law.

In practical advice books, like anything else in life, there are no guarantees of results. This book is not intended for use as a source of medical advice. All readers are advised to seek services of competent professionals in the medical field as needed.

ISBN-13: 978-1987859034

ISBN-10: 1987859030

Contents

Introduction 7

PART ONE:
The Science of Getting Rich/Wattles 13
1. The Right to be Rich 15
2. There is a Science of Getting Rich 20
3. Is Opportunity Monopolized 26
4. The First Principle in the Science of Getting Rich 32
5. Increasing Life 40
6. How Riches Come to You 48
7. Gratitude 55
8. Thinking in a Certain Way 61
9. How to Use the Will 67
10. Further Use of the Will 74
11. Acting in the Certain Way 82
12. Efficient Action 90
13. Getting into the Right Business 97
14. The Impression of Increase 103
15. The Advancing Man 109
16. Some Cautions and Concluding Observations 115
17. Summary of the Science of Getting Rich 122

PART TWO:
Action Plan/Doyd 125
1. Your Money Mindset 127
2. Your Desires and Talents 137
3. Work Goals 142
4. Uncertainty 148
5. Other People 156
6. Your Work Day 160
7. Working with the Law of Attraction 174

8. A Summary of Your Action Plan	169
Conclusion	171
About the Authors	173

Introduction

by Elizabeth N. Doyd

I have read countless books on the law of attraction on wealth. While each book has taught me something new or provided a different angle on how or why it works, when I finally read *The Science of Getting Rich*, something clicked.

What I love about this book over other popular books based on positive thinking and law of attraction is that it's simple and practical. The book itself is short and written in an accessible style, with the kind of wisdom that almost sounds like common sense.

Like many people, I was introduced to the power of thought after reading Rhonda Byrnes's *The Secret* and *The Power*. In order for this stuff to work, I only had to meditate really hard on visualizing the money that I wanted to receive and my bank account would be full—simple, right?

Well, yes and no. It's one thing to learn about the law of attraction, but another to master it. Yes, I have manifested things using the power of thought, but a lot more went into it than simply visualizing. The steps that I took was in line with the system taught in this book, even though I had not been aware of it at the time.

When it comes to wealth, many of us have blockages because we've been conditioned to feel a certain way about money: "money is the root of all evil", "rich people are ruining society", "money is hard to make", and countless other beliefs we've absorbed from others.

The truth is, money is a blessing—that is, if you earn it the right way and use it the right way. To obtain it, there is work on your part. What is the work? Exactly what God does: creation. Creating More Life.

Your creations must give value to others beyond the dollar amount that they've paid for it; whatever you're offering must benefit others in order than you benefit.

Our path to wealth is only complicated when our negative programming from years of conditioning gets in our way. But *The Science of Getting Rich* is so practical that as long as you follow this plan, your old belief system will start to fall away as you go forward.

There is no rush in getting there, no competition to worry about, and no lack mentality to bring you down when you learn to get rich as a science.

Wattles emphasizes that you don't need to be a genius to be a success. Everyone has the rudimentary skills they need already available within them. Along the way, the skills and talents can be developed further, and teachers will come forth at the right time (when the student is ready).

This is reassuring for those who believe that only the blessed and talented are deemed for great things. The truth is, we all have great potential; everyone has the power to attain what they want. If you have the desire to do something, the ability to do so already exists.

In Part One of this book, I present to you Wattles's original and unabridged book with his timeless teachings from 1910. His daughter Florence once stated that he had lived every page of his teachings. Born into poverty, he followed his own system to become a famous and well-respected author he envisioned himself to be. His books have certainly helped and inspired many people, including Rhonda Byrnes, who went on to write *The Secret* after being given this book by her daughter during a tough period in her life.

The Science of Getting Rich Action Plan

In Part Two, I take Wattles's seemingly abstract concepts and turn them into practical lessons to apply to your own life. With my extensive study of spirituality, along with my own personal experience of successes and failures, I'm able to give you guidance in layman's terms and clear up any confusions you may have.

Wattles's teachings are simplified further into 7 different topics. There are 48 questions to ask yourself so that you can get the most out of this work. Write down your responses as honestly as possible. Your answers will help you create a personalized and powerful action plan.

You can write in a notebook, a journal, or on a computer—whatever is easiest and most comfortable for you.

As for the final plan, have it written or printed out on one sheet of paper so that you can refer to it whenever you feel you need some guidance to stay on track.

Ultimately, the person who is guiding you is *you*. Nobody knows your life, your desires, your goals and worries better than you do, and you already have all the answers available within you. Writing is a way of drawing it out.

You might be surprised by some of your responses when you start writing, especially when you allow yourself to let your thoughts flow on the page with no self-analysis and judgment.

The process is not as difficult or daunting as you may think. In fact, it's fun. When you discover how you really feel about money and what you really want out of life, it's thrilling to know that whatever you want already exists for the taking.

While Wattles's book explains his system in detail, I will boil it down to an even simpler formula: Thoughts, Action & Faith.

Thoughts: When you have a burning desire to achieve something, the successful outcome already exists. And when you make the decision to achieve something, there's no need for long meditations, rituals, witchcraft or any of the other stuff you might've read from other books. Just by knowing what you want to achieve and making the decision to go for it, you have already set the plans in motion to obtain it.

Action: Take the first step in the direction of your goal. If you're unsure what step to take, just take a step. As long as you take your first step, opportunities will be presented to you along the way that would not be if you had not made the decision to move out of your comfort zone. Every day, do the best work that you can with no hurry, pressure or self-criticism.

Faith: There is no such thing as failure. What appears to be setbacks are only guideposts to help you along to an even better path. If you dwell on your fears, doubts and competition, you'll fall back from that high vibration that is above the competitive field. Cultivate gratitude. Faith will guide you where you need to go.

This book is for anyone who is serious about putting their thoughts into action in order to reach their dreams and live the life that they deserve.

Let's get started.

— Elizabeth N. Doyd

Elizabeth N. Doyd

PART ONE:
The Science of Getting Rich

by Wallace D. Wattles

The Science of Getting Rich Action Plan

Chapter One
THE RIGHT TO BE RICH

Whatever may be said in praise of poverty, the fact remains that it is not possible to live a really complete or successful life unless one is rich. No one can rise to his greatest possible height in talent or soul development unless he has plenty of money; for to unfold the soul and to develop talent he must have many things to use, and he cannot have these things unless he has money to buy them with.

A person develops in mind, soul, and body by making use of things, and society is so organized that they must have money in order to become the possessor of things; therefore, the basis of all advancement for man must be the science of getting rich.

The Science of Getting Rich Action Plan

The object of all life is development; and everything that lives has an inalienable right to all the development it is capable of attaining.

Man's right to life means his right to have the free and unrestricted use of all the things which may be necessary to his fullest mental, spiritual, and physical unfoldment; or, in other words, his right to be rich.

In this book, I shall not speak of riches in a figurative way; to be really rich does not mean to be satisfied or contented with a little. No man ought to be satisfied with a little if he is capable of using and enjoying more. The purpose of Nature is the advancement and unfoldment of life; and everyone should have all that can contribute to the power, elegance, beauty, and richness of life; to be content with less is sinful.

The man who owns all he wants for the living of all the life he is capable of living is rich; and no man who has not plenty of money can have all he wants. Life has advanced so far, and become so complex, that even the most ordinary man or woman requires a great amount of wealth in order to live in a manner that even approaches completeness. Every person naturally wants to become all that they are capable of becoming; this desire to realize innate possibilities is inherent in human nature; we cannot help wanting to be all that we can be. Success in life is becoming what you want to be; you can become what you want to be only by making use of things, and you can have the free use of things only as you become rich enough to buy them. To understand the science of getting rich is therefore the most essential of all knowledge.

There is nothing wrong in wanting to get rich. The desire for riches is really the desire for a richer, fuller, and more abundant life; and that desire is praiseworthy. The man who does not desire to live more abundantly is abnormal, and so the man who does not desire to have money enough to buy all he wants is abnormal.

There are three motives for which we live; we live for the body, we live for the mind, and we live for the soul. No one of these is better or holier than the other; all are alike desirable, and no one of the three – body, mind, or soul – can live fully if either of the others is cut short of full life and expression. It is not right or noble to live only for the soul and deny mind or body; and it is wrong to live for the intellect and deny body or soul.

We are all acquainted with the loathsome consequences of living for the body and denying both mind and soul; and we see that real life means the complete expression of all that a person can give forth through body, mind, and soul. Whatever he can say, no one can be really happy or satisfied unless his body is living fully in its every function, and unless the same is true of his mind and his soul. Wherever there is unexpressed possibility, or function not performed, there is unsatisfied desire. Desire is possibility seeking expression or function seeking performance.

Man cannot live fully in body without good food, comfortable clothing, and warm shelter; and without freedom from excessive toil. Rest and recreation are also necessary to his physical life.

One cannot live fully in mind without books and time to study them, without opportunity for travel and observation, or without intellectual companionship.

To live fully in mind he must have intellectual recreations, and must surround himself with all the objects of art and beauty he is capable of using and appreciating.

To live fully in soul, a person must have love; and love is denied fullest expression by poverty.

A man's highest happiness is found in the bestowal of benefits on those he loves; love finds its most natural and spontaneous expression in giving. The individual who has nothing to give cannot fill his place as a spouse or parent, as a citizen, or as a human being. It is in the use of material things that a person finds full life for his body, develops his mind, and unfolds his soul. It is therefore of supreme importance to each individual to be rich.

It is perfectly right that you should desire to be rich; if you are a normal man or woman you cannot help doing so. It is perfectly right that you should give your best attention to the Science of Getting Rich, for it is the noblest and most necessary of all studies. If you neglect this study, you are derelict in your duty to yourself, to God and humanity; for you can render to God and humanity no greater service than to make the most of yourself.

Chapter Two
THERE IS A SCIENCE OF GETTING RICH

There is a science to getting rich, and it is an exact science, like algebra or arithmetic. There are certain laws which govern the process of acquiring riches; once these laws are learned and obeyed by any man, he will get rich with mathematical certainty.

The ownership of money and property comes as a result of doing things in a certain way; those who do things in this Certain Way, whether on purpose or accidentally, get rich; while those who do not do things in this Certain Way, no matter how hard they work or how able they are, remain poor.

It is a natural law that like causes always produce like effects; and, therefore, any man or woman who learns to do things in this certain way will infallibly get rich.

That the above statement is true is shown by the following facts:

Getting rich is not a matter of environment, for if it were, all the people in certain neighborhoods would become wealthy; the people of one city would all be rich, while those of other towns would all be poor; or the inhabitants of one state would roll in wealth, while those of an adjoining state would be in poverty.

But everywhere we see rich and poor living side by side, in the same environment, and often engaged in the same vocations. When two people are in the same locality, and in the same business, and one gets rich while the other remains poor, it shows that getting rich is not, primarily, a matter of environment. Some environments may be more favorable than others, but when two men in the same business are in the same neighborhood, and one gets rich while the other fails, it indicates that getting rich is the result of doing things in a Certain Way.

And further, the ability to do things in this certain way is not due solely to the possession of talent, for many people who have great talent remain poor, while others who have very little talent get rich.

The Science of Getting Rich Action Plan

Studying the people who have become rich, we find that they are an average lot in all respects, having no greater talents and abilities than other men. It is evident that they do not get rich because they possess talents and abilities that other men have not, but because they happen to do things in a Certain Way.

Getting rich is not the result of saving, or "thrift"; many very penurious people are poor, while free spenders often get rich.

Nor is getting rich due to doing things which others fail to do; for two men in the same business often do almost exactly the same things, and one gets rich while the other remains poor or becomes bankrupt.

From all these things, we must come to the conclusion that getting rich is the result of doing things in a Certain Way.

If getting rich is the result of doing things in a Certain Way, and if like causes always produce like effects, then any man or woman who can do things in that way can become rich, and the whole matter is brought within the domain of exact science.

The question arises here, whether this Certain Way may not be so difficult that only a few may follow it. This cannot be true, as we have seen, so far as natural ability is concerned. Talented people get rich, and blockheads get rich; intellectually brilliant people get rich, and very stupid people get rich; physically strong people get rich, and weak and sickly people get rich.

Some degree of ability to think and understand is, of course, essential; but in so far as natural ability is concerned, any man or woman who has sense enough to read and understand these words can certainly get rich.

Also, we have seen that it is not a matter of environment. Location counts for something; one would not go to the heart of the Sahara and expect to do successful business. Getting rich involves the necessity of dealing with people and of being where there are people to deal with; and if these people are inclined to deal in the way you want to deal, so much the better. But that is about as far as environment goes.

If anybody else in your town can get rich, so can you; and if anybody else in your state can get rich, so can you.

Again, it is not a matter of choosing some particular business or profession. People get rich in every business and in every profession; while their next door neighbors in the very same vocation remain in poverty.

It is true that you will do best in a business that you like, and which is congenial to you; and if you have certain talents which are well developed,

The Science of Getting Rich Action Plan

you will do best in a business which calls for the exercise of those talents.

Also, you will do best in a business which is suited to your locality; an ice cream parlor would do better in a warm climate than in Greenland, and a salmon fishery will succeed better in the northwest than in Florida, where there are no salmon.

But, aside from these general limitations, getting rich is not dependent upon your engaging in some particular business, but upon your learning to do things in a Certain Way. If you are now in business, and anybody else in your locality is getting rich in the same business, while you are not getting rich, it is simply because you are not doing things in the same Way that the other person is doing them.

No one is prevented from getting rich by lack of capital. True, as you get capital the increase becomes more easy and rapid; but one who has capital is already rich, and does not need to consider how to become so. No matter how poor you may be, if you begin to do things in the Certain Way you will begin to get rich; and you will begin to have capital. The getting of capital is a part of the process of getting rich; and it is a part of the result which invariably follows the doing of things in the Certain Way. You may be the poorest person on the continent and be deeply in debt; you may have neither friends, influence, nor resources; but if you begin to do things in this way, you must infallibly begin to get rich, for like causes must produce like effects. If you have no capital, you can get capital; if you are in the wrong business, you can get into the right business; if you are in the wrong location, you can go to the right location; and you can do so by beginning in your present business and in your present location to do things in the Certain Way which causes success.

Chapter Three
IS OPPORTUNITY MONOPOLIZED?

No man is kept poor because opportunity has been taken away from him; because other people have monopolized the wealth, and have put a fence around it. You may be shut off from engaging in business in certain lines, but there are other channels open to you. Probably it would be hard for you to get control of any of the great railroad systems; that field is pretty well monopolized. But the electric railway business is still in its infancy, and offers plenty of scope for enterprise; and it will be but a very few years until traffic and transportation through the air will become a great industry, and in all its branches will give employment to hundreds of thousands, and perhaps to millions, of people. Why not turn your attention to the development of aerial transportation, instead of competing with J.J. Hill and others for a chance in the steam railway world?

It is quite true that if you are a workman in the employ of the steel trust you have very little chance of becoming the owner of the plant in which you work; but it is also true that if you will commence to act in a Certain Way, you can soon leave the employ of the steel trust; you can buy a farm of from ten to forty acres, and engage in business as a producer of foodstuffs. There is great opportunity at this time for men who will live upon small tracts of land and cultivate the same intensively; such men will certainly get rich. You may say that it is impossible for you to get the land, but I am going to prove to you that it is not impossible, and that you can certainly get a farm if you will go to work in a Certain Way.

At different periods the tide of opportunity sets in different directions, according to the needs of the whole, and the particular stage of social evolution which has been reached. At present, in America, it is setting toward agriculture and the allied industries and professions. To-day, opportunity is open before the factory worker in his line. It is open before the business man who supplies the farmer more than before the one who supplies the factory worker; and before the professional man who waits upon the farmer more than before the one who serves the working class.

The Science of Getting Rich Action Plan

There is abundance of opportunity for the man who will go with the tide, instead of trying to swim against it.

So the factory workers, either as individuals or as a class, are not deprived of opportunity. The workers are not being "kept down" by their masters; they are not being "ground" by the trusts and combinations of capital. As a class, they are where they are because they do not do things in a Certain Way. If the workers of America chose to do so, they could follow the example of their brothers in Belgium and other countries, and establish great department stores and co-operative industries; they could elect men of their own class to office, and pass laws favoring the development of such co-operative industries; and in a few years they could take peaceable possession of the industrial field.

The working class may become the master class whenever they will begin to do things in a Certain Way; the law of wealth is the same for them as it is for all others. This they must learn; and they will remain where they are as long as they continue to do as they do. The individual worker, however, is not held down by the ignorance or the mental slothfulness of his class; he can follow the tide of opportunity to riches, and this book will tell him how.

No one is kept in poverty by a shortness in the supply of riches; there is more than enough for all. A palace as large as the capitol at Washington might be built for every family on earth from the building material in the United States alone; and under intensive cultivation this country would produce wool, cotton, linen, and silk enough to cloth each person in the world finer than Solomon was arrayed in all his glory; together with food enough to feed them all luxuriously.

The visible supply is practically inexhaustible; and the invisible supply really is inexhaustible.

Everything you see on earth is made from one original substance, out of which all things proceed.

New forms are constantly being made, and older ones are dissolving, but all are shapes assumed by One Thing.

There is no limit to the supply of Formless Stuff, or Original Substance. The universe is made out of it; but it was not all used in making the universe. The spaces in, through, and between the forms of the visible universe are permeated and filled with the Original Substance; with the formless Stuff; with the raw material of all things. Ten thousand times as much as has been made might still be made, and even then we should not have exhausted the supply of universal raw material. No one, therefore, is poor because nature is poor or because there is not enough to go around.

Nature is an inexhaustible storehouse of riches; the supply will never run short. Original Substance is alive with creative energy, and is constantly producing more forms. When the supply of building material is exhausted, more will be produced; when the soil is exhausted so that food stuffs and materials for clothing will no longer grow upon it, it will be renewed or more soil will be made. When all the gold and silver has been dug from the earth, if man is still in such a stage of social development that it needs gold and silver, more will be produced from the Formless. The Formless Stuff responds to the needs of mankind; it will not let the world be without any good thing.

This is true of man collectively; the race as a whole is always abundantly rich, and if individuals are poor, it is because they do not follow the Certain Way of doing things which makes the individual rich.

The Formless Stuff is intelligent; it is stuff which thinks. It is alive, and is always impelled toward more life. It is the natural and inherent impulse of life to seek to live more; it is the nature of intelligence to enlarge itself, and of consciousness to seek to extend its boundaries and find fuller expression. The universe of forms has been made by Formless Living Substance, throwing itself into form in order to express itself more fully.

The universe is a great Living Presence, always moving inherently toward more life and fuller functioning. Nature is formed for the advancement of life; its impelling motive is the increase of life. For this cause, everything which can possibly minister to life, is bountifully provided; there can be no lack unless God is to contradict himself and nullify his own works.

You are not kept poor by lack in the supply of riches; it is a fact which I shall demonstrate a little farther on that even the resources of the Formless Supply are at the command of the man or woman will act and think in a certain way.

Chapter Four
THE FIRST PRINCIPLE IN THE SCIENCE OF GETTING RICH

Thought is the only power which can produce tangible riches from the Formless Substance. The stuff from which all things are made is a substance which thinks, and a thought of form in this substance produces the form.

Original Substance moves according to its thoughts; every form and process you see in nature is the visible expression of a thought in Original Substance. As the Formless Stuff thinks of a form, it takes that form; as it thinks of a motion, it makes that motion. That is the way all things were created. We live in a thought world, which is part of a thought universe. The thought of a moving universe extended throughout formless substance, and the Thinking Stuff moving according to that thought, took the form of systems of planets, and maintains that form. Thinking Substance takes the form of its thought, and moves according to the thought. Holding the idea of a circling system of suns and worlds, it takes the form of these bodies, and moves them as it thinks. Thinking the form of a slow-growing oak tree, it moves accordingly, and produces the tree, though centuries may be required to do the work. In creating, the Formless seems to move according to the lines of motion it has established; the thought of an oak tree does not cause the instant formation of a full-grown tree, but it does start in motion the forces which will produce the tree, along established lines of growth.

Every thought of form, held in thinking Substance, causes the creation of the form, but always, or at least generally, along lines of growth and action already established.

The thought of a house of a certain construction, if it were impressed upon Formless Substance, might not cause the instant formation, of the house; but it would cause the turning of creative energies already working in trade and commerce into such channels as to result in the speedy building of the house. And if there were no existing channels through which the creative energy could work, then the house would be formed directly from primal substance, without waiting for the slow processes of the organic and inorganic world.

The Science of Getting Rich Action Plan

No thought of form can be impressed upon Original Substance without causing the creation of the form.

Man is a thinking center, and can originate thought. All the forms that man fashions with his hands must first exist in his thought; he cannot shape a thing until he has thought that thing. And so far man has confined his efforts wholly to the work of his hands; he has applied manual labor to the world of forms, seeking to change or modify those already existing. He has never thought of trying to cause the creation of new forms by impressing his thoughts upon Formless Substance.

When a man has a thought-form, he takes material from the forms of nature, and makes an image of the form which is in his mind. He has, so far, made little or no effort to co-operate with Formless Intelligence; to work "with the Father." He has not dreamed that he can "do what he seeth the Father doing." Man reshapes and modifies existing forms by manual labor; he has given no attention to the question whether he may not produce things from Formless Substance by communicating his thoughts to it. We propose to prove that he may do so; to prove that any man or woman may do so; and to show how. As our first step, we must lay down three fundamental propositions.

First, we assert that there is one original formless stuff, or substance, from which all things are made. All the seemingly many elements are but different presentations of one element; all the many forms found in organic and inorganic nature are but different shapes, made from the same stuff. And this stuff is thinking stuff; a thought held in it produces the form of the thought. Thought, in thinking substance, produces shapes. Man is a thinking center, capable of original thought; if man can communicate his thought to original thinking substance, he can cause the creation, or formation, of the thing he thinks about. To summarize this:

There is a thinking stuff from which all things are made, and which, in its original state, permeates, penetrates, and fills the interspaces of the universe.

A thought, in this substance, Produces the thing that is imaged by the thought.

Man can form things in his thought, and, by impressing his thought upon formless substance, can cause the thing he thinks about to be created.

It may be asked if I can prove these statements; and without going into details, I answer that I can do so, both by logic and experience.

Reasoning back from the phenomena of form and thought, I come to one original thinking substance; and reasoning forward from this thinking substance, I come to a man's power to cause the formation of the thing he thinks about.

The Science of Getting Rich Action Plan

And by experiment, I find the reasoning true; and this is my strongest proof.

If one person who reads this book gets rich by doing what it tells him to do, that is evidence in support of my claim; but if every person who does what it tells him to do gets rich, that is positive proof until someone goes through the process and fails. The theory is true until the process fails; and this process will not fail, for everyone who does exactly what this book tells him to do will get rich.

I have said that people get rich by doing things in a Certain Way; and in order to do so, people must become able to think in a certain way.

A man's way of doing things is the direct result of the way he thinks about things.

To do things in the way you want to do them, you will have to acquire the ability to think the way you want to think; this is the first step toward getting rich.

To think what you want to think is to think TRUTH, regardless of appearances.

Every man has the natural and inherent power to think what he wants to think, but it

requires far more effort to do so than it does to think the thoughts which are suggested by appearances. To think according to appearances is easy; to think truth regardless of appearances is laborious, and requires the expenditure of more power than any other work we are called upon to perform.

There is no labor from which most people shrink as they do from that of sustained and consecutive thought; it is the hardest work in the world. This is especially true when truth is contrary to appearances. Every appearance in the visible world tends to produce a corresponding form in the mind which observes it; and this can only be prevented by holding the thought of the TRUTH.

To look upon the appearance of disease will produce the form of disease in your own mind, and ultimately in your body, unless you hold the thought of the truth, which is that there is no disease; it is only an appearance, and the reality is health.

To look upon the appearances of poverty will produce corresponding forms in your own mind, unless you hold to the truth that there is no poverty; there is only abundance.

To think health when surrounded by the appearances of disease, or to think riches when in the midst of appearances of poverty, requires power; but he who acquires this power becomes a MASTER MIND. He can conquer fate; he can have what he wants.

This power can only be acquired by getting hold of the basic fact which is behind all appearances; and that fact is that there is one Thinking

The Science of Getting Rich Action Plan

Substance, from which and by which all things are made.

Then we must grasp the truth that every thought held in this substance becomes a form, and that man can so impress his thoughts upon it as to cause them to take form and become visible things.

When we realize this, we lose all doubt and fear, for we know that we can create what we want to create; we can get what we want to have, and can become what we want to be. As a first step toward getting rich, you must believe the three fundamental statements given previously in this chapter; and in order to emphasize them, I repeat them here:

There is a thinking stuff from which all things are made, and which, in its original state, permeates, penetrates, and fills the interspaces of the universe.

A thought, in this substance, Produces the thing that is imaged by the thought.

Man can form things in his thought, and, by impressing his thought upon formless substance, can cause the thing he thinks about to be created.

You must lay aside all other concepts of the universe than this monistic one; and you must dwell upon this until it is fixed in your mind, and has become your habitual thought. Read these statements over and over again; fix every word upon your memory, and meditate upon them until you firmly believe what they say. If a doubt comes to you, cast it as a sin. Do not listen to any arguments against this idea; do not go to churches or lectures where a contrary concept of things is taught or preached. Do not read magazines or books which teach a different idea; if you get mixed up in your faith, all your efforts will be in vain.

Do not ask why these things are true, nor speculate as to how they can be true; simply take them on trust.

The science of getting rich begins with the absolute acceptance of this.

Chapter Five
INCREASING LIFE

You must get rid of the last vestige of the old idea that there is a Deity whose will it is that you should be poor, or whose purposes may be served by keeping you in poverty.

The Intelligent Substance which is All, and in All, and which lives in All and lives in you, is a consciously Living Substance. Being a consciously living substance, It must have the nature and inherent desire of every living intelligence for increase of life. Every living thing must continually seek for the enlargement of its life, because life, in the mere act of living, must increase itself.

A seed, dropped into the ground, springs into activity, and in the act of living produces a hundred more seeds; life, by living, multiplies itself. It is forever Becoming More: it must do so, if it continues to be at all.

Intelligence is under this same necessity for continuous increase. Every thought we think makes it necessary for us to think another thought; consciousness is continually expanding. Every fact we learn leads us to the learning of another fact; knowledge is continually increasing. Every talent we cultivate brings to the mind the desire to cultivate another talent; we are subject to the urge of life, seeking expression, whichever ever drives us on to know more, to do more, and to be more.

In order to know more, do more, and be more we must have more; we must have things to use, for we learn, and do, and become, only by using things. We must get rich, so that we can live more.

The desire for riches is simply the capacity for larger life seeking fulfillment; every desire is the effort of an unexpressed possibility to come into action. It is power seeking to manifest which causes desire. That which makes you want more money is the same as that which makes the plant grow; it is Life, seeking fuller expression.

The One Living Substance must be subject to this inherent law of all life; it is permeated with the desire to live more; that is why it is under the necessity of creating things.

The One Substance desires to live more in you; hence it wants you to have all the things you can use.

The Science of Getting Rich Action Plan

It is the desire of God that you should get rich. He wants you to get rich because he can express himself better through you if you have plenty of things to use in giving him expression. He can live more in you if you have unlimited command of the means of life.

The universe desires you to have everything you want to have.

Nature is friendly to your plans.

Everything is naturally for you.

Make up your mind that this is true.

It is essential, however, that your purpose should harmonize with the purpose that is in All.

You must want real life, not mere pleasure or sensual gratification. Life is the performance of function; and the individual really lives only when he performs every function, physical, mental, and spiritual, of which he is capable, without excess in any.

You do not want to get rich in order to live swinishly, for the gratification of animal desires; that is not life. But the performance of every physical function is a part of life, and no one lives completely who denies the impulses of the body, a normal and healthful expression.

You do not want to get rich solely to enjoy mental pleasures, to get knowledge, to gratify ambition, to outshine others, to be famous. All these are a legitimate part of life, but the person who lives for the pleasures of the intellect alone will only have a partial life, and he will never be satisfied with his lot.

You do not want to get rich solely for the good of others, to lose yourself for the salvation of mankind, to experience the joys of philanthropy and sacrifice. The joys of the soul are only a part of life, and they are no better or nobler than any other part.

You want to get rich in order that you may eat, drink, and be merry when it is time to do these things; in order that you may surround yourself with beautiful things, see distant lands, feed your mind, and develop your intellect; in order that you may love others and do kind things, and be able to play a good part in helping the world to find truth.

But remember that extreme altruism is no better and no nobler than extreme selfishness; both are mistakes.

Get rid of the idea that God wants you to sacrifice yourself for others, and that you can secure his favor by doing so; God requires nothing of the kind.

What God wants is that you should make the most of yourself, for yourself, and for others; and you can help others more by making the most of yourself than in any other way.

The Science of Getting Rich Action Plan

You can make the most of yourself only by getting rich; so it is right and praiseworthy that you should give your first and best thought to the work of acquiring wealth.

Remember, however, that the desire of Substance is for all, and its movements must be for more life to all; it cannot be made to work for less life to any, because it is equally in all, seeking riches and life.

Intelligent Substance will make things for you, but it will not take things away from someone else and give them to you. You must get rid of the thought of competition. You are to create, not to compete for what is already created.

You do not have to take anything away from anyone.

You do not have to drive sharp bargains.

You do not have to cheat, or to take advantage. You do not need to let anyone work for you for less than he earns.

You do not have to covet the property of others, or to look at it with wishful eyes; no man has anything of which you cannot have the like, and that without taking what he has away from him.

You are to become a creator, not a competitor; you are going to get what you want, but in such a way that when you get it every other man will have more than he has now.

I am aware that there are those who get a vast amount of money by proceeding in direct opposition to the statements in the paragraph above, and may add a word of explanation here. Men of the plutocratic type, who become very rich, do so sometimes purely by their extraordinary ability on the plane of competition; and sometimes they unconsciously relate themselves to Substance in its great purposes and movements for the general upbuilding through industrial evolution. Rockefeller, Carnegie, Morgan, et al., have been the unconscious agents of the Supreme in the necessary work of systematizing and organizing productive industry; and in the end, their work will contribute immensely toward increased life for all. Their day is nearly over; they have organized production, and will soon be succeeded by the agents of the multitude, who will organize the machinery of distribution.

The multi-millionaires are like the monster reptiles of the prehistoric eras; they play a necessary part in the evolutionary process, but the same Power which produced them will dispose of them. And it is well to bear in mind that they have never been really rich; a record of the private lives of most of this class will show that they have really been most abject and wretched.

Riches secured on the competitive plane are never satisfactory and permanent; they are yours to-day and another's tomorrow. Remember, if you are to become rich in a scientific and certain way, you must rise entirely out of competitive thought. You must never think for a moment that the supply is limited. Just as soon as you begin to think that all the money is being "cornered" and controlled by others, and that you must exert yourself to get laws passed to stop this process, and so on; in that moment, you drop into the competitive mind, and your power to cause creation is gone for the time being; and what is worse, you will probably arrest the creative movements you have already instituted.

KNOW that there are countless millions of dollars' worth of gold in the mountains of the earth, not yet brought to light; and know that if there were not, more would be created from Thinking Substance to supply your needs.

KNOW that the money you need will come, even if it is necessary for a thousand men to be led to the discovery of new gold mines to-morrow.

Never look at the visible supply; look always at the limitless riches in Formless Substance, and KNOW that they are coming to you as fast as you can receive and use them. Nobody, by cornering the visible supply, can prevent you from getting what is yours.

So never allow yourself to think for an instant that all the best building spots will be taken before you get ready to build your house, unless you hurry. Never worry about the trusts and combines, and get anxious for fear they will soon come to own the whole earth. Never get afraid that you will lose what you want because some other person "beats you to it." That cannot possibly happen; you are not seeking anything that is possessed by anybody else; you are causing what you want to be created from formless Substance, and the supply is without limits. Stick to the formulated statement:

There is a thinking stuff from which all things are made, and which, in its original state, permeates, penetrates, and fills the interspaces of the universe.

A thought, in this substance, produces the thing that is imaged by the thought.

Man can form things in his thought, and, by impressing his thought upon formless substance, can cause the thing he thinks about to be created.

Chapter Six
HOW RICHES COME TO YOU

When I say that you do not have to drive sharp bargains, I do not mean that you do not have to drive any bargains at all or that you are above the necessity for having any dealings with your fellow men. I mean that you will not need to deal with them unfairly; you do not have to get something for nothing, but can give to every person more than you take from him.

You cannot give everyone more in cash market value than you take from him, but you can give him more in use value than the cash value of the thing you take from him. The paper, ink, and other material in this book may not be worth the money you pay for it; but if the ideas suggested by it bring you thousands of dollars, you have not been wronged by those who sold it to you; they have given you a great use value for a small cash value.

Let us suppose that I own a picture by one of the great artists, which, in any civilized society, is worth thousands of dollars. I take it to Baffin Bay, and by "salesmanship" induce an Eskimo to give a bundle of furs worth $500 for it. I have really wronged him, for he has no use for the picture; it has no use value to him; it will not add to his life.

But suppose I give him a gun worth $50 for his furs; then he has made a good bargain. He has use for the gun; it will get him many more furs and much food; it will add to his life in every way. It will make him rich.

When you rise from the competitive to the creative plane, you can scan your business transactions very strictly, and if you are selling any person anything which does not add more to his life than the thing he give you in exchange, you can afford to stop it. You do not have to beat anybody in business. And if you are in a business which does beat people, get out of it at once.

Give everyone more in use value than you take from him in cash value; then you are adding to the life of the world by every business transaction.

If you have people working for you, you must take from them more in cash value than you pay them in wages, but you can so organize your business that

The Science of Getting Rich Action Plan

it will be filled with the principle of advancement, and so that each employee who wishes to do so may advance a little every day.

You can make your business do for your employees what this book is doing for you. You can so conduct your business that it will be a sort of ladder, by which every employee who will take the trouble may climb to riches himself; and given the opportunity, if he will not do so it is not your fault.

And finally, just because you are to cause the creation of your riches from Formless Substance which permeates all your environment, it does not follow that they are to take shape from the atmosphere and come into being before your eyes.

If you want a sewing machine, for instance, I do not mean to tell you that you are to impress the thought of a sewing machine on Thinking Substance until the machine is formed without hands, in the room where you sit ,or elsewhere. But if you want a sewing machine, hold the mental image of it with the most positive certainty that it is being made or is on its way to you. After once forming the thought, have the most absolute and unquestioning faith that the sewing machine is coming; never think of it, or speak of it, in any other way than as being sure to arrive. Claim it as already yours.

It will be brought to you by the power of the Supreme Intelligence, acting upon the minds of men. If you live in Maine, it may be that a person will be brought from Texas or Japan to engage in some transaction which will result in your getting what you want.

If so, the whole matter will be as much to that person's advantage as it is to yours.

Do not forget for a moment that the Thinking Substance is through all, in all, communicating with all, and can influence all. The desire of Thinking Substance for fuller life and better living has caused the creation of all the sewing machines already made; and it can cause the creation of millions more, and will, whenever people set it in motion by desire and faith, and by acting in a certain way.

You can certainly have a sewing machine in your house; and it is just as certain that you can have any other thing or things which you want, and which you will use for the advancement of your own life and the lives of others.

You need not hesitate about asking largely; "it is your Father's pleasure to give you the kingdom," said Jesus.

Original Substance wants to live all that is possible in you, and wants you to have all that you can use and will use for the living of the most abundant life.

If you fix upon your consciousness the fact that your desire for the possession of riches is one with the desire of Omnipotence for more complete expression, your faith becomes invincible.

Once I saw a little boy sitting at a piano, vainly trying to bring harmony out of the keys; and I saw that he was grieved and provoked by his inability to play real music. I asked him the cause of his vexation, and he answered, "I can feel the music in me, but I can't make my hands go right." The music in him was the URGE of Original Substance, containing all the possibilities of all life, all that there is of music was seeking expression through the child.

God, the One Substance, is trying to live and do and enjoy things through humanity. He is saying, "I want hands to build wonderful structures, to play divine harmonies, to paint glorious pictures; I want feet to run my errands, eyes to see my beauties, tongues to tell mighty truths and to sing marvelous songs," and so on.

All that there is of possibility is seeking expression through people. God wants those who can play music to have pianos and every other instrument, and to have the means to cultivate their talents to the fullest extent; He wants those who can appreciate beauty to be able to surround themselves with beautiful things; He wants those who can discern truth to have every opportunity to travel and observe; He wants those who can appreciate dress to be beautifully clothed, and those who can appreciate good food to be luxuriously fed.

He wants all these things because it is Himself that enjoys and appreciates them; they are his creation. It is God who wants to play, and sing, and enjoy beauty, and proclaim truth, and wear fine clothes, and eat good foods. "It is God that worketh in you to will and to do," said Paul.

The desire you feel for riches is the infinite, seeking to express Himself in you as He sought to find expression in the little boy at the piano.

So you need not hesitate to ask largely.

Your part is to focalize and express that desire to God.

This is a difficult point with most people; they retain something of the old idea that poverty and self-sacrifice are pleasing to God. They look upon poverty as a part of the plan, a necessity of nature. They have the idea that God has finished His work, and made all that He can make, and that the majority of people must stay poor because there is not enough to go around. They hold to so much of this erroneous thought that they feel ashamed to ask for wealth; they try not to want more than a very modest competence, just enough to make them fairly comfortable.

I recall now the case of one student who was told that he must get in mind a clear picture of the things he desired, so that the creative thought of them might be impressed on Formless Substance. He was a very poor man, living in a rented house, and having only what he earned from day to day; and he could not grasp the fact that all wealth was his. So, after thinking the matter over, he decided that he might reasonably ask for a new rug for the floor of his best room, and an anthracite coal stove to heat the house during the cold weather. Following the instructions given in this book, he obtained these things in a few months; and then it dawned upon him that he had not asked enough. He went through the house in which he lived, and planned all the improvements he would like to make in it; he mentally added a bay window here and a room there, until it was complete in his mind as his ideal home; and then he planned its furnishings.

Holding the whole picture in his mind, he began living in the Certain Way and moving toward what he wanted; and he owns the house now, and is rebuilding it after the form of his mental image. And now, with still larger faith, he is going on to get greater things. It has been unto him according to his faith, and so it is with you and with all of us.

Chapter Seven
GRATITUDE

The illustrations given in the last chapter will have conveyed to the reader the fact that the first step toward getting rich is to convey the idea of your wants to the Formless Substance.

This is true, and you will see that in order to do so it becomes necessary to relate yourself to the Formless Intelligence in a harmonious way.

To secure this harmonious relation is a matter of such primary and vital importance that I shall give some space to its discussion here, and give you instructions which, if you will follow them, will be certain to bring you into perfect unity of mind with God.

The whole process of mental adjustment and atonement can be summed up in one word, gratitude.

The Science of Getting Rich Action Plan

First, you believe that there is one Intelligent Substance, from which all things proceed; second, you believe that this Substance gives you everything you desire; and third, you relate yourself to it by a feeling of deep and profound gratitude.

Many people who order their lives rightly in all other ways are kept in poverty by their lack of gratitude. Having received one gift from God, they cut the wires which connect them with him by failing to make acknowledgment.

It is easy to understand that the nearer we live to the source of wealth, the more wealth we shall receive; and it is easy also to understand that the soul that is always grateful lives in closer touch with God than the one which never looks to Him in thankful acknowledgment.

The more gratefully we fix our minds on the Supreme when good things come to us, the more good things we will receive, and the more rapidly they will come; and the reason simply is that the mental attitude of gratitude draws the mind into closer touch with the source from which the blessings come.

If it is a new thought to you that gratitude brings your whole mind into closer harmony with the creative energies of the universe, consider it well, and you will see that it is true. The good things you have already have come to you along the line of obedience to certain laws. Gratitude will lead your mind out along the ways by which things come; and it will keep you in close harmony with creative thought and prevent you from falling into competitive thought.

Gratitude alone can keep you looking toward the All, and prevent you from falling into the error of thinking of the supply as limited; and to do that would be fatal to your hopes.

There is a Law of Gratitude, and it is absolutely necessary that you should observe the law if you are to get the results you seek.

The law of gratitude is the natural principle that action and reaction are always equal and in opposite directions.

The grateful outreaching of your mind in thankful praise to the Supreme is a liberation or expenditure of force; it cannot fail to reach that to which it addressed, and the reaction is an instantaneous movement toward you.

"Draw nigh unto God, and he will draw nigh unto you." That is a statement of psychological truth.

And if your gratitude is strong and constant, the reaction in Formless Substance will be strong and continuous; the movement of the things you want will be always toward you. Notice the grateful attitude that Jesus took; how He always seems to be saying, "I thank thee, Father, that thou hearest me." You cannot exercise much power without gratitude; for it is gratitude that keeps you connected with Power.

But the value of gratitude does not consist solely in getting you more blessings in the future. Without gratitude you cannot long keep from dissatisfied thought regarding things as they are.

The moment you permit your mind to dwell with dissatisfaction upon things as they are, you begin to lose ground. You fix attention upon the common, the ordinary, the poor, the squalid, and the mean; and your mind takes the form of these things. Then you will transmit these forms or mental images to the Formless, and the common, the poor, the squalid, and the mean will come to you.

To permit your mind to dwell upon the inferior is to become inferior and to surround yourself with inferior things.

On the other hand, to fix your attention on the best is to surround yourself with the best, and to become the best.

The Creative Power within us makes us into the image of that to which we give our attention. We are of Thinking Substance, and thinking substance always takes the form of that which it thinks about.

The grateful mind is constantly fixed upon the best; therefore it tends to become the best; it takes the form or character of the best, and will receive the best.

Also, faith is born of gratitude. The grateful mind continually expects good things, and expectation becomes faith. The reaction of gratitude upon one's own mind produces faith; and every outgoing wave of grateful thanksgiving increases faith. The person who has no feeling of gratitude cannot long retain a living faith, and without a living faith you cannot get rich by the creative method, as we shall see in the following chapters.

It is necessary, then, to cultivate the habit of being grateful for every good thing that comes to you; and to give thanks continuously.

And because all things have contributed to your advancement, you should include all things in your gratitude.

Do not waste a lot of time thinking or talking about the short-comings or wrong actions of those in power. Their organization of the world has created your opportunity; all you get really comes to you because of them.

Do not rage against corrupt politicians; if it were not for politicians we should fall into anarchy and your opportunity would be greatly lessened.

God has worked a long time and very patiently to bring us up to where we are in industry and government, and He is going right on with His work. There is not the least doubt that He will do away with plutocrats, trust magnates, captains of industry, and politicians as soon as they can be spared; but in the meantime, behold they are all very good. Remember that they are all helping to arrange the lines of transmission along which your riches will come to you, and be grateful to them all. This will bring you into harmonious relations with the good in everything, and the good in everything will move toward you.

Chapter Eight
THINKING IN A CERTAIN WAY

Turn back to chapter 6 and read again the story of the man who formed a mental image of his house, and you will get a fair idea of the initial step toward getting rich. You must form a clear and definite mental picture of what you want; you cannot transmit an idea unless you have it yourself.

You must have it before you can give it; and many people fail to impress Thinking Substance because they have themselves only a vague and misty concept of the things they want to do, to have, or to become.

It is not enough that you should have a general desire for wealth "to do good with"; everybody has that desire.

It is not enough that you should have a wish to travel, see things, live more, etc. Everybody has those desires also. If you were going to send a wireless message to a friend, you would not send the letters of the alphabet in their order, and let him construct the message for himself; nor would you take words at random from the dictionary. You would send a coherent sentence, one which meant something. When you try to impress your wants upon Substance, remember that it must be done by a coherent statement; you must know what you want and be specific and definite. You can never get rich, or start the creative power into action, by sending out unformed longings and vague desires.

Go over your desires just as the man I have described went over his house; see just what you want, and get a clear mental picture of it as you wish it to look when you get it.

That clear mental picture you must have continually in mind, as the sailor has in mind the port toward which he is sailing the ship, you must keep your face toward it all the time. You must no more lose sight of it than the steersman loses sight of the compass.

It is not necessary to take exercises in concentration, nor to set apart special times for prayer and affirmation, nor to "go into the silence," nor to do occult stunts of any kind. Some of these things are well enough, but all you need is to know what you want and to want it badly enough so that it will stay in your thoughts.

Spend as much of your leisure time as you can in contemplating your picture, but no one needs to take exercises to concentrate his mind on a thing which he really wants; it is the things you do not really care about which require effort to fix your attention upon them.

And unless you really want to get rich, so that the desire is strong enough to hold your thoughts directed to the purpose as the magnetic pole holds the needle of the compass, it will hardly be worth while for you to try to carry out the instructions given in this book.

The methods set forth here are for people whose desire for riches is strong enough to overcome mental laziness and the love of ease, and make them work.

The more clear and definite you make your picture then, and the more you dwell upon it, bringing out all its delightful details, the stronger your desire will be; and the stronger your desire, the easier it will be to hold your mind fixed upon the picture of what you want.

Something more is necessary, however, than merely to see the picture clearly. If that is all you do, you are only a dreamer, and will have little or no power for accomplishment.

Behind your clear vision must be the purpose to realize it; to bring it out in tangible expression.

And behind this purpose must be an invincible and unwavering FAITH that the thing is already yours; that it is "at hand" and you have only to take possession of it.

Live in the new house, mentally, until it takes form around you physically. In the mental realm, enter at once into full enjoyment of the things you want.

"Whatsoever things ye ask for when ye pray, believe that ye receive them, and ye shall have them," said Jesus.

See the things you want as if they were actually around you all the time; see yourself as owning and using them. Make use of them in imagination just as you will use them when they are your tangible possessions. Dwell upon your mental picture until it is clear and distinct, and then take the Mental Attitude of Ownership toward everything in that picture. Take possession of it, in mind, in the full faith that it is actually yours. Hold to this mental ownership; do not waiver for an instant in the faith that it is real.

And remember what was said in a proceeding chapter about gratitude; be as thankful for it all the time as you expect to be when it has taken form. The person who can sincerely thank God for the things which as yet he owns only in imagination, has real faith. He will get rich; he will cause the creation of whatever he wants.

You do not need to pray repeatedly for things you want; it is not necessary to tell God about it every day.

"Use not vain repetition as the heathen do," said Jesus to his pupils, "for your Father knoweth the ye have need of these things before ye ask Him."

Your part is to intelligently formulate your desire for the things which make for a larger life, and to get these desire arranged into a coherent whole; and then to impress this Whole Desire upon the Formless Substance, which has the power and the will to bring you what you want.

You do not make this impression by repeating strings of words; you make it by holding the vision with unshakable PURPOSE to attain it, and with steadfast FAITH that you do attain it.

The answer to prayer is not according to your faith while you are talking, but according to your faith while you are working. You cannot impress the mind of God by having a special Sabbath day set apart to tell Him what you want, and then forgetting Him during the rest of the week. You cannot impress Him by having special hours to go into your closet and pray, if you then dismiss the matter from your mind until the hour of prayer comes again.

Oral prayer is well enough, and has its effect, especially upon yourself, in clarifying your vision and strengthening your faith; but it is not your oral petitions which get you what you want. In order to get rich you do not need a "sweet hour of prayer"; you need to "pray without ceasing." And by prayer I mean holding steadily to your vision, with the purpose to cause its creation into solid form, and the faith that you are doing so.

"Believe that ye receive them."

The whole matter turns on receiving, once you have clearly formed your vision. When you have formed it, it is well to make an oral statement, addressing the Supreme in reverent prayer; and from that moment on you must, in mind, receive what you ask for. Live in the new house; wear the fine clothes; ride in the automobile; go on the journey, and confidently plan for greater journeys. Think and speak of all the things you have asked for in terms of actual present ownership. Imagine an environment, and a financial condition exactly as you want them, and live all the time in that imaginary environment and financial condition. Mind, however, that you do not do this as a mere dreamer and castle builder; hold to the FAITH that the imaginary is being realized and to your PURPOSE to realize it. Remember that it is faith and purpose in the use of the imagination which make the difference between the scientist and the dreamer. And having learned this fact, it is here that you must learn the proper use of the Will.

Chapter Nine
HOW TO USE THE WILL

To set about getting rich in a scientific way, you do not try to apply your will power to anything outside of yourself.

You have no right to do so, anyway.

It is wrong to apply your will to other men and women, in order to get them to do what you wish done.

It is as flagrantly wrong to coerce people by mental power as it is to coerce them by physical power. If compelling people by physical force to do things for you reduces them to slavery, compelling them by mental means accomplishes exactly the same thing; the only difference is in methods. If taking things from people by physical force is robbery, them taking things by mental force is robbery also; there is no difference in principle.

You have no right to use your will power upon another person, even "for his own good"; for you do not know what is for his good. The science of getting rich does not require you to apply power or force to any other person, in any way whatsoever. There is not the slightest necessity for doing so; indeed, any attempt to use your will upon others will only tend to defeat your purpose.

You do not need to apply your will to things, in order to compel them to come to you.

That would simply be trying to coerce God, and would be foolish and useless, as well as irreverent.

You do not have to try to compel God to give you good things, any more than you have to use your will power to make the sun rise.

You do not have to use your will power to conquer an unfriendly deity, or to make stubborn and rebellious forces do your bidding.

Substance is friendly to you, and is more anxious to give you what you want than you are to get it.

To get rich, you need only to use your will power upon yourself.

When you know what to think and do, then you must use your will to compel yourself to think and do the right things. That is the legitimate use of the will in getting what you want – to use it in holding yourself to the right course. Use your will to keep yourself thinking and acting in the Certain Way.

Do not try to project your will, or your thoughts, or your mind out into space, to "act" on things or people.

Keep your mind at home; it can accomplish more there than elsewhere.

Use your mind to form a mental image of what you want, and to hold that vision with faith and purpose; and use your will to keep your mind working in the Right Way.

The more steady and continuous your faith and purpose, the more rapidly you will get rich because you will make only POSITIVE impressions upon Substance; and you will not neutralize or offset them by negative impressions.

The picture of your desires, held with faith and purpose, is taken up by the Formless, and permeates it to great distances – throughout the universe, for all we know.

As this impression spreads, all things are set moving toward its realization; every living thing, every inanimate thing, and the things yet uncreated, are stirred toward bringing into being that which you want. All force begins to be exerted in that direction; all things begin to move toward you. The minds of people, everywhere, are influenced toward doing the things necessary to the fulfilling of your desires, and they work for you, unconsciously.

The Science of Getting Rich Action Plan

But you can check all this by starting a negative impression in the Formless Substance. Doubt or unbelief is as certain to start a movement away from you as faith and purpose are to start one toward you. It is by not understanding this that most people who try to make use of "mental science" in getting rich make their failure. Every hour and moment you spend in giving heed to doubts and fears, every hour you spend in worry, every hour in which your soul is possessed by unbelief, sets a current away from you in the whole domain of intelligent Substance. All the promises are unto them that believe, and unto them only.

Notice how insistent Jesus was upon this point of belief; and now you know the reason why.

Since belief is all important, it behooves you to guard your thoughts; and as your beliefs will be shaped to a very great extent by the things you observe and think about, it is important that you should command your attention.

And here the will comes into use; for it is by your will that you determine upon what things your attention shall be fixed.

If you want to become rich, you must not make a study of poverty.

Things are not brought into being by thinking about their opposites. Health is never to be attained by studying disease and thinking about disease;

righteousness is not to be promoted by studying sin and thinking about sin; and no one ever got rich by studying poverty and thinking about poverty.

Medicine as a science of disease has increased disease; religion as a science of sin has promoted sin, and economics as a study of poverty will fill the world with wretchedness and want.

Do not talk about poverty; do not investigate it, or concern yourself with it. Never mind what its causes are; you have nothing to do with them.

What concerns you is the cure.

Do not spend your time in so-called charitable work, or charity movements; all charity only tends to perpetuate the wretchedness it aims to eradicate. I do not say that you should be hard-hearted or unkind, and refuse to hear the cry of need; but you must not try to eradicate poverty in any of the conventional ways. Put poverty behind you, and put all that pertains to it behind you, and "make good."

Get rich; that is the best way you can help the poor.

And you cannot hold the mental image which is to make you rich if you fill your mind with pictures of poverty. Do not read books or papers which give circumstantial accounts of the wretchedness of the tenement dwellers, of the horrors of child labor, and so on. Do not read anything which fills your mind with gloomy images of want and suffering.

You cannot help the poor in the least by knowing about these things; and the wide-spread knowledge of them does not tend at all to do away with poverty.

What tends to do away with poverty is not the getting of pictures of poverty into your mind, but getting pictures of wealth into the minds of the poor.

You are not deserting the poor in their misery when you refuse to allow your mind to be filled with pictures of that misery.

Poverty can be done away with, not by increasing the number of well-to-do people who think about poverty, but by increasing the number of poor people who purpose with faith to get rich.

The poor do not need charity; they need inspiration. Charity only sends them a loaf of bread to keep them alive in their wretchedness, or gives them an entertainment to make them forget for an hour or two; but inspiration can cause them to rise out of their misery. If you want to help the poor, demonstrate to them that they can become rich; prove it by getting rich yourself.

The only way in which poverty will ever be banished from this world is by getting a large and constantly increasing number of people to practice the teachings of this book.

People must be taught to become rich by creation, not by competition.

Every person who becomes rich by competition throws down behind him the ladder by which he rises, and keeps others down; but every person who gets rich by creation opens a way for thousands to follow, and inspires them to do so.

You are not showing hardness of heart or an unfeeling disposition when you refuse to pity poverty, see poverty, read about poverty, or think or talk about it, or to listen to those who do talk about it. Use your will power to keep your mind OFF the subject of poverty, and to keep it fixed with faith and purpose ON the vision of what you want.

Chapter Ten
FURTHER USE OF THE WILL

You cannot retain a true and clear vision of wealth if you are constantly turning your attention to opposing pictures, whether they be external or imaginary.

Do not tell of your past troubles of a financial nature, if you have had them, do not think of them at all. Do not tell of the poverty of your parents or the hardships of your early life; to do any of these things is to mentally class yourself with the poor for the time being, and it will certainly check the movement of things in your direction.

"Let the dead bury their dead," as Jesus said.

Put poverty and all things that pertain to poverty completely behind you.

You have accepted a certain theory of the universe as being correct, and are resting all your hopes of happiness on its being correct; and what can you gain by giving heed to conflicting theories?

Do not read religious books which tell you that the world is soon coming to an end; and do not read the writing of muckrakers and pessimistic philosophers who tell you that it is going to the devil.

The world is not going to the devil; it is going to God.

It is a wonderful Becoming.

True, there may be a good many things in existing conditions which are disagreeable; but what is the use of studying them when they are certainly passing away, and when the study of them only tends to check their passing and keep them with us? Why give time and attention to things which are being removed by evolutionary growth, when you can hasten their removal only by promoting the evolutionary growth as far as your part of it goes?

No matter how horrible in seeming may be the conditions in certain countries, sections, or places, you waste your time and destroy your own chances by dwelling on them.

You should interest yourself in the world's becoming rich.

Think of the riches the world is coming into, instead of the poverty it is growing out of; and bear in mind that the only way in which you can assist the world in growing rich is by growing rich yourself through the creative method—not the competitive one.

Give your attention wholly to riches; ignore poverty.

Whenever you think or speak of those who are poor, think and speak of them as those who are becoming rich, as those who are to be congratulated rather than pitied. Then they and others will catch the inspiration, and begin to search for the way out.

Because I say that you are to give your whole time and mind and thought to riches, it does not follow that you are to be sordid or mean.

To become really rich is the noblest aim you can have in life, for it includes everything else. On the competitive plane, the struggle to get rich is a Godless scramble for power over others, but when we come into the creative mind, all this is changed.

All that is possible in the way of greatness, and soul, of service and lofty endeavor, comes by way of getting rich; all is made possible by the use of things.

If you lack for physical health, you will find that the attainment of it is conditional on your getting rich.

Only those who are emancipated from financial worry, and who have the means to live a care-free existence and follow hygienic practices, can have and retain health.

Moral and spiritual greatness is possible only to those who are above the competitive battle for existence; and only those who are becoming rich on the plane of creative thought are free from the degrading influences of competition. If your heart is set on domestic happiness, remember that love flourishes best where there is refinement, a high level of thought, and freedom from corrupting influences; and these are to be found only where riches are attained by the exercise of creative thought, without strife or rivalry.

You can aim at nothing so great or noble, I repeat, as to become rich; and you must fix your attention upon your mental picture of riches, to the exclusion of all that may tend to dim or obscure the vision.

You must learn to see the underlying TRUTH in all things; you must see beneath all seemingly wrong conditions the Great One Life ever moving forward toward fuller expression and more complete happiness.

It is the truth that there is no such thing as poverty; that there is only wealth.

The Science of Getting Rich Action Plan

Some people remain in poverty because they are ignorant of the fact that there is wealth for them; and these can best be taught by showing them the way to affluence in your own person and practice.

Others are poor because, while they feel that there is a way out, they are too intellectually indolent to put forth the mental effort necessary to find that way and travel it; and for these, the very best thing you can do is to arouse their desire by showing them the happiness that comes from being rightly rich.

Others still are poor because, while they have some notion of science, they have become so swamped and lost in the maze of metaphysical and occult theories that they do not know which road to take. They try a mixture of many systems and fail in all. For these, again, the very best thing to do is to show the right way in your own person and practice; an ounce of doing things is worth a pound of theorizing.

The very best thing you can do for the whole world is to make the most of yourself.

You can serve God and humanity in no more effective way than by getting rich; that is, if you get rich by the creative method and not by the competitive one.

Another thing. We assert that this book gives in detail the principles of the science of getting rich;

and if that is true, you do not need to read any other book upon the subject. This may sound narrow and egotistical, but consider: There is no more scientific method of computation in mathematics than by addition, subtraction, multiplication, and division; no other method is possible. There can be but one shortest distance between two points. There is only one way to think scientifically, and that is to think in the way that leads by the most direct and simple route to the goal. No one has yet formulated a briefer or less complex "system" than the one set forth herein; it has been stripped of all non-essentials. When you commence on this, lay all others aside; put them out of your mind altogether.

Read this book every day; keep it with you; commit it to memory, and do not think about other "systems" and theories. If you do, you will begin to have doubts, and to be uncertain and wavering in your thought; and then you will begin to make failures.

After you have made good and become rich, you may study other systems as much as you please; but until you are quite sure that you have gained what you want, do not read anything on this line but this book, unless it be the authors mentioned in the Preface.

And read only the most optimistic comments on the world's news; those in harmony with your picture.

The Science of Getting Rich Action Plan

Also, postpone your investigations into the occult. Do not dabble in the theosophy, Spiritualism, or kindred studies. It is very likely that the dead is still alive, and are near; but if they are, let them alone; mind your own business.

Wherever the spirits of the dead may be, they have their own work to do, and their own problems to solve; and we have no right to interfere with them. We cannot help them, and it is very doubtful whether they can help us, or whether we have any right to trespass upon their time if they can. Let the dead and the hereafter alone, and solve your own problem: get rich. If you begin to mix with the occult, you will start mental cross-currents which will surely bring your hopes to shipwreck. Now, this and the preceding chapters have brought us to the following statement of basic facts:

There is a thinking stuff from which all things are made, and which, in its original state, permeates, penetrates, and fills the interspaces of the universe.

A thought, in this substance, Produces the thing that is imaged by the thought.

A person can form things in his thought, and, by impressing his thought upon formless substance, can cause the thing he thinks about to be created.

In order to do this, a person must pass from the competitive to the creative mind; he must form a clear mental picture of the things he wants, and hold this picture in his thoughts with the fixed PURPOSE to get what he wants, and the unwavering FAITH that he does get what he wants, closing his mind against all that may tend to shake his purpose, dim his vision, or quench his faith.

And in addition to all this, we shall now see that he must live and act in a Certain Way.

Chapter Eleven
ACTING IN THE CERTAIN WAY

Thought is the creative power, or the impelling force which causes the creative power to act; thinking in a Certain Way will bring riches to you, but you must not rely upon thought alone, paying no attention to personal action. That is the rock upon which many otherwise scientific metaphysical thinkers meet shipwreck – the failure to connect thought with personal action.

We have not yet reached the stage of development, even supposing such a stage to be possible, in which a person can create directly from Formless Substance without nature's processes or the work of human hands; man must not only think, but his personal action must supplement his thought.

By thought you can cause the gold in the hearts of the mountains to be impelled toward you; but it will not mine itself, refine itself, coin itself into double eagles, and come rolling along the roads, seeking its way into your pocket.

Under the impelling power of the Supreme Spirit, people's affairs will be so ordered that someone will be led to mine the gold for you; other people's business transactions will be so directed that the gold will be brought toward you, and you must so arrange your own business affairs that you may be able to receive it when it comes to you. Your thought makes all things, animate and inanimate, work to bring you what you want; but your personal activity must be such that you can rightly receive what you want when it reaches you. You are not to take it as charity, nor to steal it; you must give every man more in use value than he gives you in cash value.

The scientific use of thought consists in forming a clear and distinct mental image of what you want; in holding fast to your purpose to get what you want, and in realizing with grateful faith that you do get what you want.

Do not try to "project" your thought in any mysterious or occult way, with the idea of having it go out and do things for you; that is wasted effort and will weaken your power to think with sanity.

The action of thought in getting rich is fully explained in the preceding chapters; your faith and purpose positively impress your vision upon

Formless Substance, which has THE SAME DESIRE FOR MORE LIFE THAN YOU HAVE; and this vision, received from you, sets all the creative forces at work IN AND THROUGH THEIR REGULAR CHANNELS OF ACTION, but directed toward you. It is not your part to guide or supervise the creative process; all you have to do with that is to retain your vision, stick to your purpose, and maintain your faith and gratitude.

But you must act in a Certain Way, so that you can appropriate what is yours when it comes to you; so that you can meet the things you have in your picture, and put them in their proper places as they arrive. You can really see the truth of this. When things reach you, they will be in the hands of others, who will ask an equivalent for them.

And you can only get what is yours by giving the other person what is his.

Your pocketbook is not going to be transformed into a Fortunata's purse, which shall be always full of money without effort on your part.

This is the crucial point in the science of getting rich; right here, where thought and personal action must be combined. There are very many people who, consciously or unconsciously, set the creative forces in action by the strength and persistence of their desires, but who remain poor because they do not provide for the reception of the thing they want when it comes.

By thought, the thing you want is brought to you; by action, you receive it.

Whatever your action is to be, it is evident that you must act NOW. You cannot act in the past, and it is essential to the clearness of your mental vision that you dismiss the past from your mind. You cannot act in the future, for the future is not here yet. And you cannot tell how you will want to act in any future contingency until that contingency has arrived.

Because you are not in the right environment or the right business now, do not think that you must postpone action until you get into the right business or environment. And do not spend time in the present taking thought as to the best course in possible future emergencies; have faith in your ability to meet any emergency when it arrives.

If you act in the present with your mind on the future, your present action will be with a divided mind, and will not be effective.

Put your whole mind into present action.

Do not give your creative impulse to Original Substance, and then sit down and wait for results; if you do, you will never get them. Act now. There is never any time but now, and there never will be any time but now. If you are ever to begin to make ready for the reception of what you want, you must begin NOW.

The Science of Getting Rich Action Plan

And your action, whatever it is, must most likely be in your present business or employment, and must be upon the persons and things in your present environment.

You cannot act where you are not; you cannot act where you have been, and you cannot act where you are going to be; you can act only where you are.

Do not bother as to whether yesterday's work was well done or ill done; do today's work well. Do not try to do tomorrow's work now; there will be plenty of time to do that when you get to it.

Do not try, by occult or mystical means, to act on people or things that are out of your reach.

Do not wait for a change of environment, before you act; get a change of environment by action.

You can so act upon the environment in which you are now, as to cause yourself to be transferred to a better environment.

Hold with faith and purpose the vision of yourself in the better environment, but act upon your present environment with all your heart, and with all your strength, and with all your mind.

Do not spend any time in day dreaming or castle building; hold to the one vision of what you want, and act NOW.

Do not cast about seeking some new thing to do, or some strange, unusual, or remarkable action to perform as a first step toward getting rich. It is probable that your actions, at least for some time to come, will be the same ones you have been performing for some time past; but you are to begin now to perform these actions in the Certain Way, which will surely make you rich.

If you are engaged in some business, and feel that it is not the right one for you, do not wait until you get into the right business before you begin to act.

Do not feel discouraged, or sit down and lament because you are misplaced. No one is so misplaced that he cannot find the right place, and no one ever became so involved in the wrong business but that he cannot get into the right business.

Hold the vision of yourself in the right business, with the purpose to get into it, and the faith that you will get into it, and are getting into it, but ACT in your present business. Use your present business as the means of getting a better one, and use your present environment as the means of getting into a better one. Your vision of the right business, if held with faith and purpose, will cause the Supreme to move the right business toward you; and your action, if performed in the Certain Way, will cause you to move toward the business.

The Science of Getting Rich Action Plan

If you are an employee, or wage earner, and feel that you must change places in order to get what you want, do not "project" your thought into space and rely upon it to get you another job. It will probably fail to do so.

Hold the vision of yourself in the job you want while you ACT with faith and purpose on the job you have, and you will certainly get the job you want.

Your vision and faith will set the creative force in motion to bring it toward you, and your action will cause the forces in your own environment to move you toward the place you want. In closing this chapter, we will add another statement to our syllabus:

There is a thinking stuff from which all things are made, and which, in its original state, permeates, penetrates, and fills the interspaces of the universe.

A thought, in this substance, Produces the thing that is imaged by the thought.

A person can form things in his thought, and, by impressing his thought upon formless substance, can cause the thing he thinks about to be created.

In order to do this, a person must pass from the competitive to the creative mind; he must form a clear mental picture of the things he wants, and hold this picture in his thoughts with the fixed PURPOSE to get what he wants, and the unwavering FAITH that he does get what he wants, closing his mind to all that may tend to shake his purpose, dim his vision, or quench his faith.

So that he may receive what he wants when it comes, a person must act NOW upon the people and things in his present environment.

Chapter Twelve
EFFICIENT ACTION

You must use your thought as directed in previous chapters, and begin to do what you can do where you are; and you must do ALL that you can do where you are.

You can advance only by being larger than your present place; and no one is larger than his present place who leaves undone any of the work pertaining to that place.

The world is advanced only by those who more than fill their present places.

If no one quite filled his present place, you can see that there must be a going backward in everything. Those who do not quite fill their present places are dead weight upon society, government, commerce, and industry; they must be carried along by others at a great expense. The progress of the world is slowed only by those who do not fill the places they are holding; they belong to a former age and a lower stage or plane of life, and their tendency is toward degeneration. No society could advance if everyone was smaller than his place; social evolution is guided by the law of physical and mental evolution. In the animal world, evolution is caused by excess of life.

When an organism has more life than can be expressed in the functions of its own plane, it develops the organs of a higher plane, and a new species is originated.

There never would have been new species had there not been organisms which more than filled their places. The law is exactly the same for you; your getting rich depends upon your applying this principle to your own affairs.

Every day is either a successful day or a day of failure; and it is the successful days which get you what you want. If every day is a failure you can never get rich; while if every day is a success, you cannot fail to get rich.

If there is something that may be done today, and you do not do it, you have failed in so far as that thing is concerned; and the consequences may be more disastrous than you imagine.

You cannot foresee the results of even the most trivial act. You do not know the workings of all the forces that have been set moving in your behalf.

The Science of Getting Rich Action Plan

Much may be depending on your doing some simple act; and it may be the very thing which is to open the door of opportunity to very great possibilities. You can never know all the combinations which Supreme Intelligence is making for you in the world of things and of human affairs; your neglect or failure to do some small thing may cause a long delay in getting what you want.

Do, every day, ALL that can be done that day.

There is, however, a limitation or qualification of the above that you must take into account.

You are not to overwork, nor to rush blindly into your business in the effort to do the greatest

possible number of things in the shortest possible time.

You are not to try to do tomorrow's work today, nor to do a week's work in a day. It is really not the number of things you do, but the EFFICIENCY of each separate action that counts.

Every act is, in itself, either a success or a failure. Every act is, in itself, either effective and efficient or ineffective and inefficient.

Every inefficient act is a failure, and if you spend your life in doing inefficient acts, your whole life will be a failure.

The more things you do, the worse for you, if all your acts are inefficient ones.

On the other hand, every efficient act is a success in itself, and if every act of your life is an efficient one, your whole life MUST be a success.

The cause of failure is doing too many things in an inefficient manner, and not doing enough things in an efficient manner.

You will see that it is a self-evident proposition that if you do not do any inefficient acts, and if you do a sufficient number of efficient acts, you will become rich. If, now, it is possible for you to make each act an efficient one, you see again that the getting of riches is reduced to an exact science, like mathematics.

The matter turns, then, on ·the question of whether you can make each separate act a success in itself. And this you can certainly do.

You can make each act a success, because ALL power is working with you; and ALL power cannot fail.

Power is at your service; and to make each act efficient you have only to put power into it.

Every action is either strong or weak; and when every action is strong, you are acting in the Certain Way which will make you rich.

Every act can be made strong and efficient by holding your vision while you are doing it, and putting the whole power of your FAITH and PURPOSE into it.

The Science of Getting Rich Action Plan

It is at this point that the people fail who separate mental power from personal action. They use the power of mind in one place and at one time, and they act in another way in another place and at another time. So their acts are not successful in themselves; too many of them are inefficient. But if ALL power goes into every act, no matter how commonplace, every act will be a success in itself; and as in the nature of things that every success opens the way to other successes, your progress toward what you want and the progress of what you want toward you, will become increasingly rapid.

Remember that successful action is cumulative in its results. Since the desire for more life is inherent in all things, when a person begins to move toward larger life, more things attach themselves to him, and the influence of his desire is multiplied.

Do, every day, all that you can do that day, and do each act in an efficient manner.

In saying that you must hold your vision while you are doing each act, however trivial or commonplace, I do not mean to say that it is necessary at all times to see the vision distinctly to its smallest details. It should be the work of your leisure hours to use your imagination on the details of your vision and to contemplate them until they are firmly fixed upon memory. If you wish speedy results, spend practically all your spare time in this practice.

By continuous contemplation you will get the picture of what you want, even to the smallest details, so firmly fixed upon your mind, and so completely transferred to the mind of Formless Substance, that in your working hours, you need only to mentally refer to the picture to stimulate your faith and purpose and cause your best effort to be put forth. Contemplate your picture in your leisure hours until your consciousness is so full of it that you can grasp it instantly. You will become so enthused with its bright promises that the mere thought of it will call forth the strongest energies of your whole being.

Let us again repeat our syllabus, and by slightly changing the closing statements bring it to the point we have now reached.

There is a thinking stuff from which all things are made, and which, in its original state, permeates, penetrates, and fills the interspaces of the universe.

A thought, in this substance, produces the thing that is imaged by the thought.

A person can form things in his thought, and, by impressing his thought upon formless substance, can cause the thing he thinks about to be created.

In order to do this, a person must pass from the competitive to the creative mind; he must form a clear mental picture of the things he wants, and must do, with faith and purpose, all that can be done each day, doing each separate thing in an efficient manner.

Chapter Thirteen
GETTING INTO THE RIGHT BUSINESS

*S*uccess, in any particular business, depends for one thing upon your possessing, in a well-developed state, the faculties required in that business.

Without good musical faculty no one can succeed as a teacher of music; without well-developed mechanical faculties no one can achieve great success in any of the mechanical trades; without well-developed mechanical faculties no one can achieve great success in any of the mechanical trades; without tact and the commercial faculties no one can succeed in mercantile pursuits. But to possess in a well-developed state the faculties required in your particular vocation does not insure getting rich. There are musicians who have remarkable talent, and who yet remain poor; there are blacksmiths, carpenters, and so on who have excellent mechanical ability, but who do not get rich; and there are merchants with good faculties for dealing with people who nevertheless fail.

The different faculties are tools; it is essential to have good tools, but it is also essential that the tools should be used in the Right Way. One man can take a sharp saw, a square, a good plane, and so on, and build a handsome article of furniture; another man can take the same tools and set to work to duplicate the article, but his production will be a botch. He does not know how to use good tools in a successful way.

The various faculties of your mind are the tools with which you must do the work which is to make you rich; it will be easier for you to succeed if you get into a business for which you are well equipped with mental tools.

Generally speaking, you will do best in that business which will use your strongest faculties; the one for which you are naturally "best fitted." But there are limitations to this statement, also. No one should regard his vocation as being irrevocably fixed by the tendencies with which he was born.

You can get rich in ANY business, for if you have not the right talent, you can develop that talent; it merely means that you will have to make your tools as you go along, instead of confining yourself to the use of those with which you were born. It will be EASIER for you to succeed in a vocation for which you already have the talents in a well-developed state; but you CAN succeed in any vocation, for you can develop any rudimentary talent, and there is no talent of which you have not at least the rudiment.

You will get rich most easily in terms of effort, if you do that for which you are best fitted; but you will get rich most satisfactorily if you do that which you WANT to do.

Doing what you want to do is life; and there is no real satisfaction in living if we are compelled to be forever doing something which we do not like to do, and can never do what we want to do. And it is certain that you can do what you want to do; the desire to do it is proof that you have within you the power which can do it.

Desire is a manifestation of power.

The desire to play music is the power which can play music seeking expression and development; the desire to invent mechanical devices is the mechanical talent seeking expression and development.

Where there is no power, either developed or undeveloped, to do a thing, there is never any desire to do that thing; and where there is strong desire to do a thing, it is certain proof that the power to do it is strong, and only requires to be developed and applied in the Right Way.

The Science of Getting Rich Action Plan

All other things being equal, it is best to select the business for which you have the best developed talent; but if you have a strong desire to engage in any particular line of work, you should select that work as the ultimate end at which you aim.

You can do what you want to do, and it is your right and privilege to follow the business or vocation which will be most congenial and pleasant.

You are not obliged to do what you do not like to do, and should not do it except as a means to bring you to the doing of the thing you want to do.

If there are past mistakes whose consequences have placed you in an undesirable business or environment, you may be obliged for some time to do what you do not like to do; but you can make the doing of it pleasant by knowing that it is making it possible for you to come to the doing of what you want to do.

If you feel that you are not in the right vocation, do not act too hastily in trying to get into another one. The best way, generally, to change business or environment is by growth.

Do not be afraid to make a sudden and radical change if the opportunity is presented, and you feel after careful consideration that it is the right opportunity; but never take sudden or radical action when you are in doubt as to the wisdom of doing so.

There is never any hurry on the creative plane; and there is no lack of opportunity.

When you get out of the competitive mind you will understand that you never need to act hastily. No one else is going to beat you to the thing you want to do; there is enough for all. If one space is taken, another and a better one will be opened for you a little farther on; there is plenty of time. When you are in doubt, wait. Fall back on the contemplation of your vision, and increase your faith and purpose; and by all means, in times of doubt and indecision, cultivate gratitude.

A day or two spent in contemplating the vision of what you want, and in earnest thanksgiving that you are getting it, will bring your mind into such close relationship with the Supreme that you will make no mistake when you do act.

There is a mind which knows all there is to know; and you can come into close unity with this mind by faith and the purpose to advance in life, if you have deep gratitude.

Mistakes come from acting hastily, or from acting in fear or doubt or in forgetfulness of the Right Motive, which is more life to all, and less to none.

As you go on in the Certain Way, opportunities will come to you in increasing number; and you will need to be very steady in your faith and purpose, and to keep in close touch with All Mind by reverent gratitude.

Do all that you can do in a perfect manner every day, but do it without haste, worry, or fear. Go as fast as you can, but never hurry.

Remember that in the moment you begin to hurry you cease to be a creator and become a competitor; you drop back upon the old plane again.

Whenever you find yourself hurrying, call a halt; fix your attention on the mental image of the thing you want, and begin to give thanks that you are getting it. The exercise of GRATITUDE will never fail to strengthen your faith and renew your purpose.

Chapter Fourteen
THE IMPRESSION OF INCREASE

Whether you change your vocation or not, your actions for the present must be those pertaining to the business in which you are now engaged.

You can get into the business you want by making constructive use of the business you are already established in; by doing your daily work in the Certain Way.

And in so far as your business consists in dealing with other people, whether personally or by letter, the key-thought of all your efforts must be to convey to their minds the impression of increase.

Increase is what all men and all women are seeking; it is the urge of the Formless Intelligence within them, seeking fuller expression.

The desire for increase is inherent in all nature; it is the fundamental impulse of the universe.

The Science of Getting Rich Action Plan

All human activities are based on the desire for increase; people are seeking more food, more clothes, better shelter, more luxury, more beauty, more knowledge, more pleasure – increase in something, more life. Every living thing is under this necessity for continuous advancement; where increase of life ceases, dissolution and death set in at once.

Man instinctively knows this, and therefore he is forever seeking more. This law of perpetual increase is set forth by Jesus in the parable of the talents: only those who gain more retain any; from him who hath not shall be taken away even that which he hath.

The normal desire for increased wealth is not an evil or a reprehensible thing; it is simply the desire for more abundant life; it is aspiration. And because it is the deepest instinct of their natures, all men and women are attracted to those who can give them more of the means of life.

In following the Certain Way as described in the foregoing pages, you are getting continuous increase for yourself, and you are giving it to all with whom you deal.

You are a creative center from which increase is given off to all.

Be sure of this, and convey assurance of the fact to every man, woman, and child with whom you come in contact. No matter how small the transaction, even if it be only the selling of a stick of candy to a little child, put into it the thought of increase, and make sure that the customer is impressed with the thought.

Convey the impression of advancement with everything you do, so that all people shall receive the impression that you are an Advancing Man, and that you advance all who deal with you. Even to the people whom you meet in a social way, without any thought of business, and to whom you do not try to sell anything, give the thought of increase.

You can convey this impression by holding the unshakable faith that you, yourself, are in the Way of Increase; and by letting this faith inspire, fill, and permeate every action.

Do everything that you do in the firm conviction that you are an advancing personality and that you are giving advancement to everybody.

Feel that you are getting rich, and that in so doing you are making others rich, and conferring benefits on all.

Do not boast or brag of your success or talk about it unnecessarily; true faith is never boastful.

Wherever you find a boastful person, you find one who is secretly doubtful and afraid. Simply feel the faith, and let it work out in every transaction; let every act and tone and look express the quiet assurance that you are getting rich; that you are already rich. Words will not be necessary to communicate this feeling to others; they will feel the sense of increase when in your presence, and will be attracted to you again.

You must so impress others that they will feel that in associating with you they will get increase for themselves. See that you give them a use value greater than the cash value you are taking from them.

Take an honest pride in doing this and let everybody know it; and you will have no lack of customers. People will go where they are given increase; and the Supreme, which desires increase in all, and which knows all, will move toward you men and women who have never heard of you. Your business will increase rapidly, and you will be surprised at the unexpected benefits which will come to you. You will be able from day to day to make larger combinations, secure greater advantages, and to go on into a more congenial vocation if you desire to do so.

But doing all this, you must never lose sight of your vision of what you want, or your faith and purpose to get what you want.

Let me here give you another word of caution in regard to motives.

Beware of the insidious temptation to seek for power over other people.

Nothing is so pleasant to the unformed or partially developed mind as the exercise of power or dominion over others. The desire to rule for selfish gratification has been the curse of the world. For countless ages kings and lords have drenched the earth with blood in their battles to extend their dominions; this not to seek more life for all, but to get more power for themselves.

Today, the main motive in the business and industrial world is the same: men Marshal their armies of dollars, and lay waste the lives and hearts of millions in the same mad scramble for power over others. Commercial kings, like political kings, are inspired by the lust for power.

Jesus saw in this desire for mastery the moving impulse of that evil world He sought to overthrow. Read the twenty-third chapter of Matthew, and see how He pictures the lust of the Pharisees to be called "Master," to sit in the high places, to domineer over others, and to lay burdens on the backs of the less fortunate; and note how He compares this lust for dominion with the brotherly seeking for the Common Good to which He calls His disciples.

Look out for the temptation to seek for authority, to become a "master," to be considered as one who is above the common herd, to impress others by lavish display, and so on.

The mind that seeks for mastery over others is the competitive mind; and the competitive mind is not the creative one. In order to master your environment and your destiny, it is not at all necessary that you should rule over your fellow men and, indeed, when you fall into the world's struggle for the high places, you begin to be conquered by fate and environment; and your getting rich becomes a matter of chance and speculation.

Beware of the competitive mind! No better statement of the principle of creative action can be formulated than the favorite declaration of the late "Golden Rule" Jones of Toledo: "What I want for myself, I want for everybody."

Chapter Fifteen
THE ADVANCING MAN

What I have said in the last chapter applies as well to the professional man and the wage-earner as to the man who is engaged in mercantile business.

No matter whether you are a physician, a teacher, or a clergyman, if you can give increase of life to others and make them sensible of that fact, they will be attracted to you, and you will get rich. The physician who holds the vision of himself as a great and successful healer, and who works toward the complete realization of that vision with faith and purpose, as described in former chapters, will come into such close touch with the Source of Life that he will be phenomenally successful; patients will come to him in throngs.

No one has a greater opportunity to carry into effect the teaching of this book than the practitioner of medicine; it does not matter to which of the various schools he may belong, for the principle of healing is common to all of them and may be reached by all alike. The Advancing Man in medicine, who holds to a clear mental image of himself as successful, and who obeys the laws of faith, purpose, and gratitude, will cure every curable case he undertakes, no matter what remedies he may use.

In the field of religion, the world cries out for the clergyman who can teach his hearers the true science of abundant life. He who masters the details of the science of getting rich, together with the allied sciences of being well, of being great, and of winning love, and who teaches these details from the pulpit, will never lack for a congregation. This is a gospel that the world needs; it will give increase of life, and people will hear it gladly, and give liberal support to the person who brings it to them.

What is now needed is a demonstration of the science of life from the pulpit. We want preachers who can not only tell us how, but who in their own persons will show us how. We need the preacher who will himself be rich, healthy, great, and beloved, to teach us how to attain to these things; and when he comes he will find a numerous and loyal following.

The same is true of the teacher who can inspire the children with the faith and purpose of the advancing life. He will never be "out of a job." And any teacher who has this faith and purpose can give it to his pupils; he cannot help giving it to them if it is part of his own life and practice.

What is true of the teacher, preacher, and physician is true of the lawyer, dentist, real estate agent, insurance agent – of everybody.

The combined mental and personal action I have described is infallible; it cannot fail. Every man and woman who follows these instructions steadily, perseveringly, and to the letter, will get rich. The law of the Increase of Life is as mathematically certain in its operation as the law of gravity; getting rich is an exact science.

The wage earner will find this as true of his case as of any of the others mentioned. Do not feel that you have no chance to get rich because you are working where there is no visible opportunity for advancement, where wages are small and the cost of living high. Form your clear mental vision of what you want, and begin to act with faith and purpose.

Do all the work you can do, every day, and do each piece of work in a perfectly successful manner. Put the power of success, and the purpose to get rich, into everything that you do.

But do not do this merely with the idea of currying favor with your employer, in the hope that he, or those above you, will see your good work and advance you; it is not likely that they will do so.

The person who is merely a "good" worker, filling his place to the very best of his ability and satisfied with that, is valuable to his employer; and it is not to the employer's interest to promote him; he is worth more where he is.

To secure advancement, something more is necessary than to be too large for your place.

The person who is certain to advance is the one who is too big for his place, who has a clear concept of what he wants to be; who knows that he can become what he wants to be and who is determined to BE what he wants to be.

Do not try to more than fill your present place with a view to pleasing your employer; do it with the idea of advancing yourself. Hold the faith and purpose of increase during work hours, after work hours, and before work hours. Hold it in such a way that every person who comes in contact with you, whether foreman, fellow worker, or social acquaintance, will feel the power of purpose radiating from you; so that everyone will get the sense of advancement and increase from you. People will be attracted to you, and if there is no possibility for advancement in your present job, you will very soon see an opportunity to take another job.

There is a Power which never fails to present opportunity to the advancing personality who is moving in obedience to law.

God cannot help helping you if you act in a Certain Way; He must do so in order to help Himself.

There is nothing in your circumstances or in the industrial situation that can keep you down. If you cannot get rich working for the steel trust, you can get rich on a ten-acre farm; and if you begin to move in the Certain Way, you will certainly escape from the "clutches" of the steel trust and get on to the farm or wherever else you wish to be.

If a few thousands of its employees would enter upon the Certain Way, the steel trust would soon be in a bad plight; it would have to give its workers more opportunity, or go out of business. Nobody has to work for a trust; the trusts can keep people in so called hopeless conditions only so long as there are people who are ignorant of the science of getting rich, or too intellectually slothful to practice it.

Begin this way of thinking and acting, and your faith and purpose will make you quick to see any opportunity to better your condition.

Such opportunities will speedily come, for the Supreme, working in All, and working for you, will bring them before you.

Do not wait for an opportunity to be all that you want to be; when an opportunity to be more than you are now is presented and you feel impelled toward it, take it. It will be the first step toward a greater opportunity.

There is no such thing possible in this universe as a lack of opportunities for the person who is

living the advancing life.

It is inherent in the constitution of the cosmos that all things shall be for him and work together for his good; and he must certainly get rich if he acts and thinks in the Certain Way. So let wage earning men and women study this book with great care, and enter with confidence upon the course of action it prescribes; It will not fail.

Chapter Sixteen
SOME CAUTIONS AND CONCLUDING OBSERVATIONS

Many people will scoff at the idea that there is an exact science of getting rich; holding the impression that the supply of wealth is limited, they will insist that social and governmental institutions must be changed before even any considerable number of people can acquire a competence.

But this is not true.

It is true that existing governments keep the masses in poverty, but this is because the masses do not think and act in the Certain Way.

If the masses begin to move forward as suggested in this book, neither governments nor industrial systems can check them; all systems must be modified to accommodate the forward movement.

The Science of Getting Rich Action Plan

If the people have the Advancing Mind, have the Faith that they can become rich, and move forward with the fixed purpose to become rich, nothing can possibly keep them in poverty.

Individuals may enter upon the Certain Way at any time, and under any government, and make themselves rich; and when any considerable number of individuals do so under any government, they will cause the system to be so modified as to open the way for others.

The more men who get rich on the competitive plane, the worse for others; the more who get rich on the creative plane, the better for others. The economic salvation of the masses can only be accomplished by getting a large number of people to practice the scientific method set down in this book, and become rich. These will show others the way, and inspire them with a desire for real life, with the faith that it can be attained, and with the purpose to attain it.

For the present, however, it is enough to know that neither the government under which you live nor the capitalistic or competitive system of industry can keep you from getting rich. When you enter upon the creative plane of thought you will rise above all these things and become a citizen of another kingdom.

But remember that your thought must be held upon the creative plane; you are never for an instant to be betrayed into regarding the supply as limited or into acting on the moral level of competition.

Whenever you do fall into old ways of thought, correct yourself instantly; for when you are in the competitive mind, you have lost the cooperation of the Mind of the Whole.

Do not spend any time in planning as to how you will meet possible emergencies in the future, except as the necessary policies may affect your actions today. You are concerned with doing today's work in a perfectly successful manner, and not with emergencies which may arise tomorrow; you can attend to them as they come.

Do not concern yourself with questions as to how you shall surmount obstacles which may loom upon your business horizon, unless you can see plainly that your course must be altered today in order to avoid them.

No matter how tremendous an obstruction may appear at a distance, you will find that if you go on in the Certain Way it will disappear as you approach it, or that a way over, under, through, or around it will appear.

No possible combination of circumstances can defeat a man or woman who is proceeding to get rich along strictly scientific lines. No man or woman who obeys the law can fail to get rich, any more than one can multiply two by two and fail to get four.

Give no anxious thought to possible disasters, obstacles, panics, or unfavorable combinations of circumstances; it is time enough to meet such things when they present themselves before you in the immediate present, and you will find that every difficulty carries with it the wherewithal for its overcoming.

Guard your speech. Never speak of yourself, your affairs, or of anything else in a discouraged or discouraging way.

Never admit the possibility of failure, or speak in a way that infers failure as a possibility.

Never speak of the times as being hard, or of business conditions as being doubtful. Times may be hard and business doubtful for those who are on the competitive plane, but they can never be so for you; you can create what you want, and you are above fear.

When others are having hard times and poor business, you will find your greatest opportunities.

Train yourself to think of, and to look upon, the world as a something which is Becoming, which is growing; and to regard seeming evil as being only that which is undeveloped. Always speak in terms of advancement; to do otherwise is to deny your faith, and to deny your faith is to lose it.

Never allow yourself to feel disappointed. You may expect to have a certain thing at a certain time and not get it at that time; and this will appear to you like failure.

But if you hold to your faith you will find that the failure is only apparent.

Go on in the certain way, and if you do not receive that thing, you will receive something so much better that you will see that the seeming failure was really a great success.

A student of this science had set his mind on making a certain business combination which seemed to him at the time to be very desirable, and he worked for some weeks to bring it about. When the crucial time came, the thing failed in a perfectly inexplicable way; it was as if some unseen influence had been working secretly against him. But he was not disappointed; on the contrary, he thanked God that his desire had been overruled, and went steadily on with a grateful mind. In a few weeks an opportunity so much better came his way that he would not have made the first deal on any account; and he saw that a Mind which knew more than he knew had prevented him from losing the greater good by entangling himself with the lesser.

The Science of Getting Rich Action Plan

That is the way every seeming failure will work out for you, if you keep your faith, hold to your purpose, have gratitude, and do, every day, all that can be done that day, doing each separate act in a successful manner.

When you make a failure, it is because you have not asked for enough; keep on, and a larger thing than you were seeking will certainly come to you. Remember this.

You will not fail because you lack the necessary talent to do what you wish to do. If you go on as I have directed, you will develop all the talent that is necessary to the doing of your work.

It is not within the scope of this book to deal with the science of cultivating talent; but it is as certain and simple as the process of getting rich.

However, do not hesitate or waver for fear that when you come to any certain place you will fail for lack of ability; keep right on, and when you come to that place, the ability will be furnished to you. The same source of Ability which enabled the untaught Lincoln to do the greatest work in government ever accomplished by a single man is open to you; you may draw upon all the mind there is for wisdom to use in meeting the responsibilities which are laid upon you. Go on in full faith.

Study this book. Make it your constant companion until you have mastered all the ideas contained in it. While you are getting firmly established in this faith, you will do well to give up most recreations and pleasure; and to stay away from places where ideas conflicting with these are advanced in lectures or sermons. Do not read pessimistic or conflicting literature or get into arguments upon the matter. Spend most of your leisure time in contemplating your vision, in cultivating gratitude, and in reading this book. It contains all you need to know of the science of getting rich; and you will find all the essentials summed up in the following chapter.

Chapter Seventeen
SUMMARY OF THE SCIENCE OF GETTING RICH

There is a thinking stuff from which all things are made, and which, in its original state, permeates, penetrates, and fills the interspaces of the universe.

A thought in this substance produces the thing that is imaged by the thought.

Man can form things in his thought, and by impressing his thought upon formless substance can cause the thing he thinks about to be created.

In order to do this, man must pass from the competitive to the creative mind; otherwise he cannot be in harmony with Formless Intelligence, which is always creative and never competitive in spirit.

Man may come into full harmony with the Formless Substance by entertaining a lively and sincere gratitude for the blessings it bestows upon him. Gratitude unifies the mind of man with the intelligence of Substance, so that man's thoughts are received by the Formless. Man can remain upon the creative plane only by uniting himself with the Formless Intelligence through a deep and continuous feeling of gratitude.

Man must form a clear and definite mental image of the things he wishes to have, to do, or to become; and he must hold this mental image in his thoughts, while being deeply grateful to the Supreme that all his desires are granted to him. The man who wishes to get rich must spend his leisure hours in contemplating his Vision, and in earnest thanksgiving that the reality is being given to him. Too much stress cannot be laid on the importance of frequent contemplation of the mental image, coupled with unwavering faith and devout gratitude. This is the process by which the impression is given to the Formless and the creative forces set in motion.

The creative energy works through the established channels of natural growth, and of the industrial and social order. All that is included in his mental image will surely be brought to the person who follows the instructions given above, and whose faith does not waver. What he wants will come to him through the ways of established trade and commerce.

In order to receive his own when it is ready to come to him, man must be active; and this activity can only consist in more than filling his present place. He must keep in mind the Purpose to get rich through the realization of his mental image. And he must do, every day, all that can be done that day, taking care to do each act in a successful manner. He must give to every person a use value in excess of the cash value he receives, so that each transaction makes for more life; and he must hold the Advancing Thought so that the impression of increase will be communicated to all with whom he comes into contact.

The men and women who practice the foregoing instructions will certainly get rich; and the riches they receive will be in exact proportion to the definiteness of their vision, the fixity of their purpose, the steadiness of their faith, and the depth of their gratitude.

PART TWO: ACTION PLAN

By Elizabeth N. Doyd

The Science of Getting Rich Action Plan

1.
YOUR MONEY MINDSET

First, let's examine your relationship with money. We'll shed light on your blind spots in order to remove them.

The beliefs and attitudes we have towards money is one of our major blocks to wealth. Most of us are taught that money is evil, rich people are greedy, and that we must scrimp and save wherever we can because there isn't enough to go around. This societal attitude doesn't make it easy for us to like money, even when we have it.

The fact remains that it is not possible to live a really complete or successful life unless one is rich… No man ought to be satisfied with a little if he is capable of using and enjoying more.

The Science of Getting Rich Action Plan

1) Do you agree with Wattles's statement?

If you don't, why? Is it really your opinion, or one inherited from others around you?

2) Do you believe that you deserve to be rich?

If you grew up in a middle class household like me, maybe you've had similar experiences of walking into a fancy restaurant or an event where rich people gather, and feeling entirely out of place. When you're used to living in a certain way, it becomes your comfort zone. Some of us might not have had the experience of wealth yet in order to feel comfortable in a wealthy environment. This brings me to my next question:

3) What do you think separates you from someone who is extremely wealthy?

4) Do you really love money or do you fear it? Do you subconsciously talk yourself out of a wealthy lifestyle due to a lifetime of conditioning?

No one can rise to his greatest possible height in talent or soul development unless he has plenty of money; for to unfold the soul and to develop talent he must have many things to use, and he cannot have these things unless he has money to buy them with.

5) **What have you already been able to achieve with the help of money?** For example, perhaps you were able to receive a good education, travel, or buy a house for your family. Or maybe you were able to buy that guitar because you always wanted to learn to play music, donate to a charity that you support, or feel confident in the clothes that you love. List all of them down.

There are three motives for which we live; we live for the body, we live for the mind, and we live for the soul.

6) **How well are you taking care of your body? Are you constantly feeding your mind with positivity and wisdom? What are you doing to nourish your soul? And how does money come in to help you nourish your body, mind and soul?** For example, maybe money enables you to buy healthy food, attend yoga classes, take trips, or do other soul-fulfilling activities you otherwise wouldn't be able to.

To live fully in soul, a person must have love; and love is denied fullest expression by poverty.

7) **How would more love enter into your life with the aid of money?** For example, would you be able to spend more time with your family if you didn't have to work overtime and stress over finances? Would you be able to provide a better life for yourself and those you love? Would you be able to help improve the economy by having the money to purchase products and services of the highest quality?

No one is kept in poverty by a shortness in the supply of riches; there is more than enough for all...

8) You might intellectually understand this statement, but do you believe it? **In what ways do you feel lack in your life? How do you perpetuate this belief?** For example, do you clip coupons? Are you constantly fighting to overtake your competitors? Do you hoard items because you're afraid that there might not be enough left later on? Have you ever looked at a price tag for something you wanted and thought, "too expensive—I'm not paying that much"?

There is nothing wrong in wanting to get rich. The desire for riches is really the desire for a richer, fuller, and more abundant life; and that desire is praiseworthy. The man who does not desire to live more abundantly is abnormal, and so the man who does not desire to have money enough to buy all he wants is abnormal.

9) **In what ways have you been "abnormal" in your life?** Do you sell yourself short by making decisions based on money? Do you feel guilty for not saving enough? Do you get stressed out when you make a big purchase that you think you shouldn't? What's your definition of managing money responsibly?

You must get rid of the last vestige of the old idea that there is a Deity whose will it is that you should be poor, or whose purposes may be served by keeping you in poverty...In order to know more, do more, and be more we must have more; we must have things to use, for we learn, and do, and become, only by using things. We must get rich, so that we can live more... That which makes you want more money is the same as that which makes the plant grow; it is Life, seeking fuller expression.

10) **Do you have the belief that there is a certain righteousness in poverty?** Many artists for example have "starving artist syndrome" where they believe that living in poverty, or even sickness, brings them closer to the truth. But that is only one

truth. Being happy and rich is another truth, if you choose it.

11) Do you feel like a victim or believe that poverty is what you deserve?

If you're unsure, read this statement out loud:

MONEY COMES TO ME EASILY. I HAVE A MILLION DOLLARS IN MY BANK ACCOUNT. EVERY DAY I'M MAKING MORE AND MORE.

How did it make you feel? Note down your reactions.

It is the desire of God that you should get rich. He wants you to get rich because he can express himself better through you if you have plenty of things to use in giving him expression. He can live more in you if you have unlimited command of the means of life…The universe desires you to have everything you want to have…Nature is friendly to your plans… Everything is naturally for you…Make up your mind that this is true.

12) **What can you do now to give yourself more wealthy experiences so that you can start living the life you really desire?** Have you shied away from better restaurants because you didn't want to fork over the extra expense? Have you tried on shoes you love, but sighed with longing because it's out of your usual price range? Do you always fly economy when you have enough to fly business or first class? Have you always wanted to take a cooking class but end up telling yourself, "I don't have the money for that right now"?

Write down all the ways you can start experiencing more wealth in your life, especially things to improve the mind, body and soul. **List the things you want to do and what you want to buy to contribute to your new lifestyle.** I'm not saying to go crazy with your credit card and buy the entire mall—this might stress you out even more if you have some deep rooted beliefs and guilt about spending a lot of money when you're not used to it. Start with what is doable. If you can buy a better brand of toothpaste over the cheap tube you usually use, do it.

The only difference between you and a rich person is that they have a heck of a lot more money. The first time I flew first class, I was surprised by how ordinary the other passengers looked and behaved. They were simply used to flying comfortably while I felt guilty for spending extra money for a better seat because I had the middle-class mentality of wanting to save money. The reason I did push myself fly first class was to break out of my middle-class comfort zone and to give myself the experience of having the best.

You must want real life, not mere pleasure or sensual gratification. Life is the performance of function; and the individual really lives only when he performs every function, physical, mental, and spiritual, of which he is capable, without excess in any...You want to get rich in order that you may eat, drink, and be merry when it is time to do these things; in order that you may surround yourself with beautiful things, see distant lands, feed your mind, and develop your intellect; in order that you may love others and do kind things, and be able to play a good part in helping the world to find truth.

13) **How much money do you really want in your back account?** Don't just pick any random number that sounds high; pick an amount that would allow you to live the life that you want. List your expenses and calculate how much you need to make every month to live really well.

Maybe you just want a one-room condo, or you want a mansion and a yacht. Maybe you want enough money to travel every other month or pay your kids' tuition fees. Money=freedom. How can money help you improve EVERY area of your life?

This number can change, of course. Maybe you'll reach half your goal and feel perfectly happy with your current lifestyle, or you might want more once you reach that goal because you've formed new desires. That's perfectly fine as well.

If you want to become rich, you must not make a study of poverty...What concerns you is the cure... Get rich; that is the best way you can help the poor. What tends to do away with poverty is not the getting of pictures of poverty into your mind, but getting pictures of wealth into the minds of the poor. The poor do not need charity; they need inspiration...The only way in which poverty will ever be banished from this world is by getting a large and constantly increasing number of people to practice the teachings of this book.

14) **Can you imagine yourself as rich, and as an inspiration to those around you?** Or are you afraid of being alienated or resented by others, especially by your friends and family, for having more money? Don't be! If they can't be happy for your success, it is not your concern. Don't let other people keep you from your dreams because they are not taking the action to reach theirs.

The Science of Getting Rich Action Plan

If you need to, distance yourself from those who cannot accept your success. Some people simply do not want to see others get ahead because they're reminded of how little they are accomplishing. Just keep following your vision. Along the way, you'll attract more positive and like-minded people like you. Remember that you are doing not only yourself but the world a favor by being fabulously wealthy. Don't stay small because others are afraid to go big.

2.
YOUR DESIRES AND TALENTS

Growing up, we've been taught to be competitive in one way or another. We're graded in school and compared to each other in so many ways that we've come to measure our own worth by other people's accomplishments.

The thing is, we don't know the journey and the transformation that the other person had to go through in order to achieve their success; we only see their success and assume that it was easy or "luck" that got them there. We didn't see their struggles, internal and external, that they had to work through to make their desires a reality.

Whenever someone is successful, the desire came first. Then they took action, while not allowing any opposition (such as rejection and discouragement) to get in their way.

Here, we'll explore your true desires and what's getting in the way in making them a reality.

The Science of Getting Rich Action Plan

Generally speaking, you will do best in that business which will use your strongest faculties; the one for which you are naturally "best fitted"...It is true that you will do best in a business that you like, and which is congenial to you; and if you have certain talents which are well developed, you will do best in a business which calls for the exercise of those talents.

15) **What are you naturally good at?** List all your strengths and talents.

But there are limitations to this statement, also. No one should regard his vocation as being irrevocably fixed by the tendencies with which he was born.

16) Just because you're good at math doesn't mean that you have to be an accountant if the idea doesn't appeal to you. **What do you LIKE to do?** It can be things that you don't necessarily think you're that good at.

You can get rich in ANY business, for if you have not the right talent, you can develop that talent; it merely means that you will have to make your tools as you go along, instead of confining yourself to the use of those with which you were born. It will be EASIER for you to succeed in a vocation for which you already have the talents in a well-developed state; but you CAN succeed in any vocation, for you can develop any rudimentary talent, and there is no talent of which you have not at least the rudiment.

17) **Have you ever wanted to do something but didn't think you had the talent to succeed in it?** Wattles' statement is incredibly liberating. **Desire+taking focused action** trumps talent. This explains why there are superstar singers who can barely sing, while many who are much more vocally talented can't seem to make it past the first round of American Idol.

If you really have the *desire* to do something, you can succeed in it. Any talent can be developed along the way. **What do you really want to do?** If you're uncertain, take a look at the people you admire. What is it about them that is so inspiring? If you envy them, what is it that you envy exactly? This can give you some clues.

Getting rich is not a matter of environment, for if it were, all the people in certain neighborhoods would become wealthy...the ability to do things in this certain way is not due solely to the possession of talent, for many people who have great talent remain poor, while others who have very little talent get rich...Getting rich is not the result of saving, or "thrift"; many very penurious people are poor, while free spenders often get rich...Nor is getting rich due to doing things which others fail to do; for two men in the same business often do almost exactly the same things, and one gets rich while the other remains poor or becomes bankrupt.

18) **What excuses do you give yourself for not being rich and successful yet?** Is it because you feel you didn't have the proper education? Nurturing parents? The right connections? The right car, clothes, personality? Be aware of the limitations that you are placing on yourself. This is your "story" and it keeps you stuck.

Talented people get rich, and blockheads get rich; intellectually brilliant people get rich, and very stupid people get rich; physically strong people get rich, and weak and sickly people get rich.

19) Can you list some examples of people, either public figures or those you know, whose journey proves each of the above statements to be true?

Where there is no power, either developed or undeveloped, to do a thing, there is never any desire to do that thing; and where there is strong desire to do a thing, it is certain proof that the power to do it is strong, and only requires to be developed and applied in the Right Way.

20) Look at your list of desires. **Is it what you** *really* **want, or is it what someone else wants for you?** Were you taught by your parents, teachers or society in general to get into certain fields because it is more financially stable?

Check in with your inner self when you read each desire. How do you feel? What does your gut tell you?

The Science of Getting Rich Action Plan

3.
WORK GOALS

Now that you know how much you want to make, what your desires are and what you're good at, let's get clear on your work values.

The universe is a great Living Presence, always moving inherently toward more life and fuller functioning. Nature is formed for the advancement of life; its impelling motive is the increase of life. For this cause, everything which can possibly minister to life, is bountifully provided; there can be no lack unless God is to contradict himself and nullify his own works.

21) Find examples in your own life to support this. **Whenever you've experienced success in the past, did it contribute to More Life?** For example, did your work bring joy or inspiration to others?

Did you employ people and provide them with jobs? Did you collaborate or form creative partnerships?

Get rid of the idea that God wants you to sacrifice yourself for others, and that you can secure his favor by doing so; God requires nothing of the kind... What God wants is that you should make the most of yourself, for yourself, and for others; and you can help others more by making the most of yourself than in any other way... You can make the most of yourself only by getting rich; so it is right and praiseworthy that you should give your first and best thought to the work of acquiring wealth.

22) **Is getting rich a priority for you?** Are you willing to do everything you can to achieve your goals? Why or why not? If it's not a priority, what is?

The mind can come up with all sorts of excuses why money is not important. Churches need money, charities need money, every worthy cause has money working to their advantage. So why wouldn't you want more money in your life?

Intelligent Substance will make things for you, but it will not take things away from someone else and give them to you. You must get rid of the thought of competition. You are to create, not to compete

The Science of Getting Rich Action Plan

for what is already created....You do not have to take anything away from anyone...You do not have to drive sharp bargains...You do not have to cheat, or to take advantage. You do not need to let anyone work for you for less than he earns...You do not have to covet the property of others, or to look at it with wishful eyes; no man has anything of which you cannot have the like, and that without taking what he has away from him.

23) We are bombarded with reality shows where contestants are eliminated each week and the top "survivor" is rewarded with everything. While these shows may be entertaining to watch, you don't need to compete in real life order to be successful.

You're here to be an individual. God put a specific desire in you with the full capability to obtain your desires. If you are competing with other individuals or companies, who are they? Why are you threatened by them?

You are to become a creator, not a competitor; you are going to get what you want, but in such a way that when you get it every other man will have more than he has now...No man is kept poor because opportunity has been taken away from him; because other people have monopolized the wealth, and have put a fence around it. You may be shut off from engaging in business in certain lines, but there are other channels open to you...New forms are constantly being made, and older ones are dissolving, but all are shapes assumed by One Thing...The Formless Stuff is intelligent; it is stuff which thinks. It is alive, and is always impelled toward more life.

24) List all the ways that you're bringing More Life to others in your line of work. Do you know what your clients really want from you? How are you adapting to cater to their needs?

I do not mean that you do not have to drive any bargains at all or that you are above the necessity for having any dealings with your fellow men. I mean that you will not need to deal with them unfairly; you do not have to get something for nothing, but can give to every person more than you take from him...Give everyone more in use value than you take from him in cash value; then you are adding to the life of the world by every business transaction.

25) **Are you charging enough in your business?** Many people charge less than they deserve because they're afraid to lose business, or fear their "competition" will snatch their client or deal away from them. This is dealing on the competitive plane.

To get clear on the value of what you are offering, describe what your customers are receiving from you. How much value is in what they are receiving? Can you put a dollar figure on it? Are others in similar fields charging more or charging less? What's stopping you from charging the top rate?

When you charge what you deserve, you might lose the people who are not willing to pay your new price, but you will attract the people who will, and who will value your services more. Can you let one go for the other?

When you rise from the competitive to the creative plane, you can scan your business transactions very strictly, and if you are selling any person anything which does not add more to his life than the thing he give you in exchange, you can afford to stop it. You do not have to beat anybody in business. And if you are in a business which does beat people, get out of it at once.

26) If you're not sure whether your products or services are offering other people value, ask yourself if this is something that they would want or need. Is it something entertaining? Would it bring them joy? Does it make their life easier?

If you have people working for you, you must take from them more in cash value than you pay them in wages, but you can so organize your business that it will be filled with the principle of advancement, and so that each employee who wishes to do so may advance a little every day...You can make your business do for your employees what this book is doing for you. You can so conduct your business that it will be a sort of ladder, by which every employee who will take the trouble may climb to riches himself; and given the opportunity, if he will not do so it is not your fault.

27) Do you employ people? If so, are they advancing? Even if there is no position in your company for them to advance to, are they learning from you? Don't be afraid of losing employees if they've outgrown their current positions. Your success in business and in life depends on your ability to give More Life to others.

4. UNCERTAINTY

It's only natural when you doubt whether you can actually achieve your goals. After all, this world is designed to challenge us. If there was no "negativity", "satan", "ego", or whatever you want to call it, it would be heaven on earth and we would get everything we want in a second. Where is the fun in that?

Our job here on the physical plane is to become like God and create our own heaven on earth; we must remove our blockages and really earn our wealth, love, and happiness in order to truly appreciate it.

Whatever challenges you are facing right now, know that you are merely being tested. Once you work past it, your soul will transform more than you would've if what you wanted was handed to you on a silver platter. You covet what you earn!

There is a mind which knows all there is to know; and you can come into close unity with this mind by faith and the purpose to advance in life, if you have deep gratitude. Mistakes come from acting hastily, or from acting in fear or doubt or in forgetfulness of the Right Motive, which is more life to all, and less to none.

28) **Write down your goal, or your "Right Motive", in one sentence.**

For example, if you want success in selling a line of toys, your goal might be to see kids deriving pleasure from playing with your products (therefore producing More Life).

There is never any hurry on the creative plane; and there is no lack of opportunity....When you are in doubt, wait. Fall back on the contemplation of your vision, and increase your faith and purpose; and by all means, in times of doubt and indecision, cultivate gratitude...A day or two spent in contemplating the vision of what you want, and in earnest thanksgiving that you are getting it, will bring your mind into such close relationship with the Supreme that you will make no mistake when you do act...Do not be afraid to make a sudden and radical change if the opportunity is presented, and you feel after careful consideration that it is the right opportunity; but never take sudden or radical action when you are in doubt as to the wisdom of doing so.

29) **Is there anything that you are unsure of?** Write your question or problem down and then ask for guidance. Your mind is always working for you to give you the answers that you are seeking. Have you ever gone to sleep fretting over a problem, then woke up the next morning with an answer? You have all the answers you need already within you. You just have to draw it out by asking the right questions.

Do not spend any time in planning as to how you will meet possible emergencies in the future, except as the necessary policies may affect your actions today. You are concerned with doing today's work in a perfectly successful manner, and not with emergencies which may arise tomorrow; you can attend to them as they come...Do not concern yourself with questions as to how you shall surmount obstacles which may loom upon your business horizon, unless you can see plainly that your course must be altered today in order to avoid them.

30) **What are you worried about in your day to day life?** Write them down. These are the worries that are constantly circulating in your head.

They're hard to chase out, but you can gradually wean them out by replacing the thoughts with something positive. For example, if you're always worrying about how you're going to pay the rent on time, take a deep breath, and tell yourself, "I have more than enough money for all my needs". Write the positive equivalent for each worry that you have and repeat this to yourself when the worries descend.

Guard your speech. Never speak of yourself, your affairs, or of anything else in a discouraged or discouraging way....That is the way every seeming failure will work out for you, if you keep your faith, hold to your purpose, have gratitude, and do, every day, all that can be done that day, doing each separate act in a successful manner.

31) Do you have the bad habit of putting yourself down? Sometimes people do this because they get energy from complaining, or they want sympathy from others. Prevent yourself from doing this. Whatever temporary high you receive from venting about your frustrations won't compare to the joy you'll feel when you make your dreams a reality.

If others are asking how you are doing in your business, you can **prepare some positive responses in advance.**

For example, if someone asks if you're a success yet, and you don't feel anywhere near successful, you can say, "Yes, I'm doing very well, and certainly headed in the direction that I've envisioned."

You don't need to answer every question. Inquiries about how much you make are not considered polite anyhow. If you get these types of questions from relatives, just smile and say something vague, like "more than enough". If they still don't get the hint and keep pressing you, just ask lightly, "why so curious"? Why are they so curious? It's not their business.

When you make a failure, it is because you have not asked for enough; keep on, and a larger thing than you were seeking will certainly come to you. Remember this.

32) Have you ever thought you "failed" at something, only to have it work to your advantage later on? **Find examples of this from your own life.** Maybe you didn't get top marks on a pop quiz, but it pushed you to do really well on your exam. Or maybe you had a crush on someone who rejected you, but you went on later to date someone you like much more. Maybe you didn't get the job you wanted, but found a job that suited you better with higher pay. Find and list as many as possible.

When you failed at something, what did you learn from it?

You will not fail because you lack the necessary talent to do what you wish to do. If you go on as I have directed, you will develop all the talent that is necessary to the doing of your work.

33) Many people are uncertain of their talents. You've probably heard about great writers who actually destroyed their work because it wasn't up to their personal satisfaction. It's one thing to have high standards, but another to be so hard on yourself that you prevent yourself from releasing what you create. If God put the desire in you to do something, you owe it to world to share it. Don't worry if it's not perfect. Finish it to the best of your ability and get it out there.

What's important is that you take action. If you want to run a marathon, you can't just sit on the couch, eat cheese puffs and imagine your way into a fit body that could get you to the finish line. You must have an diet and exercise plan that would allow you to achieve this. **What skills do you think you can develop or improve to help you succeed in your field?**

Do not tell of your past troubles of a financial nature, if you have had them, do not think of them at all. Do not tell of the poverty of your parents or the hardships of your early life; to do any of these things is to mentally class yourself with the poor for the time being, and it will certainly check the movement of things in your direction...You have accepted a certain theory of the universe as being correct, and are resting all your hopes of happiness on its being correct; and what can you gain by giving heed to conflicting theories?

34) People usually have "stories" of why making money is hard for them. Maybe they grew up poor, didn't have the education they wanted, received constant rejection, etc. **What stories of hardship do you tell yourself?**

It's time to create a new story. Your past happened to teach you something. The future is yours for the making.

True, there may be a good many things in existing conditions which are disagreeable; but what is the use of studying them when they are certainly passing away, and when the study of them only tends to check their passing and keep them with us? Why give time and attention to things which are being removed by evolutionary growth, when you can hasten their removal only by promoting the evolutionary growth as far as your part of it goes?

35) Are you wasting your time dwelling on bad news? Find inspiration in good news. In every field there is someone who overcame all odds and became successful. During the financial crisis, many companies and entrepreneurs were unaffected by it. **List the success story of someone you admire. What do you think contributed to their success? Can you apply their work ethics and methods to your own work and daily routine?**

5.
OTHER PEOPLE

You probably come in contact with all sorts of people every day: people who want to do business with you, and people who want nothing to do with you; people who like what you're offering, and people who abhor it; people who are easy to get along with, and people who are much more challenging; people who are inspiring, and people who spread a negative energy to everyone they meet.

There's a right way of working with people that promotes circuitry and harmony. Wattles touches on the ethics of dealing with others beautifully in his book. Here, we'll touch on how you can get the most out of your interactions with other people in business and in your day-to-day life.

Every person who becomes rich by competition throws down behind him the ladder by which he rises, and keeps others down; but every person who gets rich by creation opens a way for thousands to follow, and inspires them to do so.

36) **If there is something that you really envy in a "competitor", note why.** This might be telling you that there's an area of your life that you must pay attention to improve.

You can either get dragged into an envious state in the wake of other people's success, or you can find them to be inspiring. The fact that they are successful doesn't take away from what's coming to you. No two businesses are exactly the same. YOU offer something special.

But you must act in a Certain Way, so that you can appropriate what is yours when it comes to you; so that you can meet the things you have in your picture, and put them in their proper places as they arrive. You can really see the truth of this. When things reach you, they will be in the hands of others, who will ask an equivalent for them.

37) Are you always worrying about how things are going to reach you? And get frustrated when it doesn't come in a certain way?

Relax. When you get worried, take a deep breath and close your eyes. Imagine yourself surrounded by gold light. Your light is like a magnet, drawing all the riches to you.

Let the universe surprise you on how your success will come to you. Be open to different opportunities and new ideas. Be open to receiving what you strived for. If you get too caught up in the HOW, let it go and focus on the final vision of your success.

Convey the impression of advancement with everything you do, so that all people shall receive the impression that you are an Advancing Man, and that you advance all who deal with you. Even to the people whom you meet in a social way, without any thought of business, and to whom you do not try to sell anything, give the thought of increase.

38) Do you only talk to people who can help you in some way? Some people do this unintentionally. Practice being the "Advancing Man/Woman" to everyone and having no agenda in your social interactions. Whether you are talking to a bum on the street, or the CEO of a large corporation, practice giving them the energy of increase.

Think of the riches the world is coming into, instead of the poverty it is growing out of; and bear in mind that the only way in which you can assist the world in growing rich is by growing rich yourself through the creative method—not the competitive one.

Whenever you think or speak of those who are poor, think and speak of them as those who are becoming rich, as those who are to be congratulated rather than pitied. Then they and others will catch the inspiration, and begin to search for the way out.

39) I know that it can be difficult to think of the world as rich and abundant when you pass beggars on the streets, or know countless friends and family members who are stressed out by their financial situations. What you can do to help them is to live the fullest life that YOU can live.

There reminds me of a quote by Rumi: "*Yesterday I was clever, so I wanted to change the world. Today I am wise, so I am changing myself.*"

Instead of pitying others who are in distress, or treating them like a negative nuisance, why not give them a smile or a kind word? It doesn't matter if they don't return it; it's their choice how they conduct themselves. But they have crossed your path for a reason. The best way you can help them is to be an inspiration.

6.
YOUR WORK DAY

Act now. There is never any time but now, and there never will be any time but now. If you are ever to begin to make ready for the reception of what you want, you must begin NOW…And your action, whatever it is, must most likely be in your present business or employment, and must be upon the persons and things in your present environment… You cannot act where you are not; you cannot act where you have been, and you cannot act where you are going to be; you can act only where you are.

40) Even though you may feel that your goal is far from your present situation, you can only start getting there from where you are now. This means that whatever you are working on now must be given your best efforts, or you must change businesses to be in the business you really want.

List all the action steps you are aware of to get to where you want to be. This includes studying, letting go of self-limiting beliefs, attending seminars, networking, etc. As you take these steps to your goal, more steps will be revealed to you, so concern yourself with what you can do now.

Use your present business as the means of getting a better one, and use your present environment as the means of getting into a better one. Your vision of the right business, if held with faith and purpose, will cause the Supreme to move the right business toward you; and your action, if performed in the Certain Way, will cause you to move toward the business...If you are an employee, or wage earner, and feel that you must change places in order to get what you want, do not "project" your thought into space and rely upon it to get you another job. It will probably fail to do so...Hold the vision of yourself in the job you want while you ACT with faith and purpose on the job you have, and you will certainly get the job you want.

41) Do you have doubts that come up when you try to envision yourself as a success? If so, what are they? When you are aware of what they are, you can actively remove them by replacing them with thoughts of certainty. The mind can be trained, you do not need to be a victim to its negatively. You are the master and you can bend your thoughts to benefit you.

The Science of Getting Rich Action Plan

Every day is either a successful day or a day of failure; and it is the successful days which get you what you want. If every day is a failure you can never get rich; while if every day is a success, you cannot fail to get rich...You are not to overwork, nor to rush blindly into your business in the effort to do the greatest possible number of things in the shortest possible time.

42) I know someone who works seven days a week from morning to night. He wants to make more money, but charges less than what he's worth because more people hire him this way. He also tends to take on last minute projects because tight deadlines give him the "high" to accelerate his work speed. His goal is "good enough", not "the best that he can do".

He makes a decent living, but imagine how much more balanced he would be if he stopped taking rush jobs and used his free time to nourish the other aspects of his life that he'd been neglecting, including his family? Imagine what would happen if he stopped taking many low-paying jobs for a few high paying jobs. What if he actually took the time and energy to put his best effort into each project?

I've presented the possibilities to him, but he doesn't want to change his habits because he has become accustomed to this way of working. He's not motivated to change because he's comfortable. This is an example of how action affects outcome. By accepting or rejecting certain things, we are showing the universe what we are willing or not willing to receive.

Don't wait until you are stressed and overloaded with work to take the right actions. **Observe in your own business or life how you are short-changing yourself.**

You are not to try to do tomorrow's work today, nor to do a week's work in a day. It is really not the number of things you do, but the EFFICIENCY of each separate action that counts.

43) **What does efficiency mean for your business?** In order to reach your goal, do you need to make a certain amount of sales in X amount of time? Do you need to hire people? Do you have to schedule your time better? Are you avoiding certain tasks because you are afraid of rejection or failure?

For example, if you want to be a nutritionist, are you going out and finding people who need your help? If getting clients/making sales is a priority, but you're filling your day with menial tasks, you're distracting yourself from your ultimate goal.

Remember that your product/service is a benefit to others, and that means you might have to get out of your comfort zone sometimes and talk to people and attract the right opportunities.

7.
WORKING WITH THE LAW OF ATTRACTION

The key to success in the Law of Attraction is holding your vision with consistency and imbuing it with positive energy (love and gratitude). You are probably aware by now of the negative fears and worries you do have. While you might not be able to get rid of them easily, you can turn away from them.

Whenever doubt begins to creep in, release it and focus on your final vision.

Read again the story of the man who formed a mental image of his house, and you will get a fair idea of the initial step toward getting rich. You must form a clear and definite mental picture of what you want; you cannot transmit an idea unless you have it yourself...When you try to impress your wants upon Substance, remember that it must be done by a coherent statement; you must know what you want and be specific and definite. You can never get rich, or start the creative power into action, by sending out unformed longings and vague desires...Live in the new house, mentally, until it takes form around you physically. In the mental realm, enter at once into full enjoyment of the things you want.

45) When Jim Carrey started his career, he used to drive up to Mulholland Drive in Los Angeles and park in a place where he could see the Hollywood lights. While sitting in his car, he used to visualize that he was the biggest star in the world, and repeated to himself, "everyone wants to work with me". He would feel what it was like to be successful.

However, he wasn't just sitting around waiting for that $10 million dollar check (that he ultimately received for The Cable Guy), he was performing as a standup comedian in as many as three clubs a night and co-creating his success with the universe.

Get specific on what you want and feel what it's like to have it. When you visualize your goals, don't envision it like you're watching yourself in a movie. BE in your own body experiencing the joyride in the new car, or admiring the view from your office, holding that big check, etc.

The more clear and definite you make your picture then, and the more you dwell upon it, bringing out all its delightful details, the stronger your desire will be; and the stronger your desire, the easier it will be to hold your mind fixed upon the picture of what you want...Something more is necessary, however, than merely to see the picture clearly. If that is all you do, you are only a dreamer, and will have little or no power for accomplishment...Remember that it is faith and purpose in the use of the imagination which make the difference between the scientist and the dreamer.

46) **What are your feelings when you imagine yourself in this life?** If you feel with LOVE and FAITH, it will be so powerful and magnetic that you will manifest faster.

You do not need to pray repeatedly for things you want; it is not necessary to tell God about it every day...You do not make this impression by repeating strings of words; you make it by holding the vision with unshakable PURPOSE to attain it, and with steadfast FAITH that you do attain it.

The Science of Getting Rich Action Plan

8. A SUMMARY OF YOUR ACTION PLAN

Write or print out this plan on one piece of paper with your answers so you can refer to it when you need to.

THE SCIENCE OF GETTING RICH ACTION PLAN

You present situation:

Your ultimate goal (purpose and $ goal):

Why do you want to make this much money?

How does your product or service give More Life to others?

First step to take towards your goal:

Skills you must improve:

The Science of Getting Rich Action Plan

What to visualize:

Positive mantras to replace negative ones:

How you're improving your mind, body and soul:

CONCLUSION

This system doesn't have to be limited to obtaining money. What other areas of your life would you like to improve?

For example, if you're having health problems, hold the vision of yourself completely healthy. Then take the first step you're aware of in remedying this situation. Maybe it's to see a specialist or doing a certain type of exercise. When you take the first step, the universe will provide other people and resources to come into your life to help with your issue.

This is a simple system that might take some effort to master. After all, the world was designed to challenge your faith. But by holding the vision of what you want, taking the action steps and having faith that you will receive it, events will unfold to help you manifest it. Sometimes you might have to drag your dark shadows of doubt and negativity behind you on the journey, but that's okay.

The Science of Getting Rich Action Plan

As long as you feel faith and gratitude 51% of the time, the universe will tip in your favor. This is called the tipping point. As long as you have more faith than doubt, you will succeed.

When those doubts come—and they will, because they are tricky buggers out to confuse you—let them come, then release them. Increase your faith and gratitude. Take deep breaths through the nose and exhale through the mouth to calm yourself down and release the worries from your body. If you can meditate or do things to quiet the mind, this will also help you master your mind.

When you follow the science, you'll reach your goals in no time.

About the Authors

Wallace D. Wattles

Born in 1860, Wallace D. Wattles was an American author whose most famous work is *The Science of Getting Rich*, which has gone on to inspire countless others, including modern-day spiritual gurus and motivational speakers. Other books by Wattles include *Health Through New Thought and Fasting, The Science of Being Great, The Science of Being Well, Making of the Man Who Can* and a novel, *Hellfire Harrison*.

Elizabeth N. Doyd

Elizabeth N. Doyd is the author of the bestselling books *Write Him Off: Journal Prompts to Heal Your Broken Heart in 30 Days*, and *Gratitude Journal: 52 Writing Prompts to Celebrate Your Wonderful Life*. She also works as a relationship expert and spiritual counselor, having studied Kabbalah, Buddhism, hypnotherapy, astrology and Reiki.

The Science of Getting Rich Action Plan

Elizabeth N. Doyd

The Science of Getting Rich Action Plan

Made in the USA
Columbia, SC
06 February 2023